ALL-PRO
WISDOM

"YOU MAY NOT BE AN ALL-PRO FOOTBALL PLAYER,
BUT YOU CAN CHOOSE TO LIVE AN ALL-PRO LIFE."
—ROGER GOODELL, NFL COMMISSIONER

ALL-PRO WISDOM

THE 7 CHOICES
THAT LEAD TO GREATNESS

SUPER BOWL CHAMPION AND NFL MAN OF THE YEAR

MATT BIRK

WITH RICH CHAPMAN

HIDDEN CREEK PUBLISHING
Mendota Heights, MN

Published by

Hidden Creek Publishing

Mendota Heights, MN

Publisher's Cataloging-in-Publication Data
Birk, Matt.
All-Pro wisdom : the seven choices that lead to greatness /
Matt Birk with Rich Chapman ;
foreword by Roger Goodell. – Mendota Heights, MN : Hidden Creek Pub., 2014.
p. ; cm.
ISBN13: 978-0-9860718-0-5
1. Wisdom. 2. Conduct of life. 3. Personality development. 4. Self-actualization (Psychology)
5. Birk, Matt. 6. Football players--United States. I. Title. II. Chapman, Rich. III. Goodell, Roger.

BJ1589.B57 2014 158.1—dc23   2013957116

Project coordination by Jenkins Group, Inc.
www.BookPublishing.com

Interior design by Yvonne Fetig Roehler

Printed in the United States of America
18   17   16   15   14   •   5   4   3   2   1

Adrianna—it is an honor.
Madison, Sydney, Ava,
Grant, Cole, and Brady—thanks
for being my kids.
—MATT

To Jayme—my inspiration.
To Nicole, Greta, Billy,
and Teddy—my joy.
—RICH

CONTENTS

FOREWORD

This book is not about football. It's about choices. Important choices made by extraordinary men who play the game of football. Each of them is an All-Pro, the best of the best, both personally and professionally. I have the pleasure of knowing Matt Birk personally. He won the Walter Payton NFL Man of the Year Award for his excellence on and off the field. Matt has represented the NFL by being more than an outstanding football player. Like all the men profiled in this book, Matt's leadership has made and will continue to make a positive influence every day in the lives of many people. When it comes to life skills, these are true impact players who have much to teach us. They exemplify an important part of what makes the NFL special.

I started my career with the NFL as an intern more than thirty years ago. My journey required hard work, perseverance, and good choices. If you want to be successful, if you want to be sure you are setting a strong foundation, then I urge you to reflect carefully on the questions posed in the pages of this book. Like me, you may not be an All-Pro football player, but each of us can choose to live an All-Pro life! You can be like Matt and the others he profiled, a person of positive impact, no matter your calling.

Our NFL mission statement includes a commitment "to provide each individual with the opportunity to achieve his or her full potential." Remember to live out the seven choices and you will be well on your way to achieving your full potential and becoming your very best!

Roger Goodell
NFL Commisssioner
January 2014

GREATNESS IS WITHIN YOUR GRASP

What a thrill it has been for me to collaborate with Matt on this project! While the Seven Choices have guided many people for many years, they are now accessible to you through the publication of our book. Matt's generosity and his relationships with the best of the best opened the doors that have allowed us to offer you this "All-Pro Guide" to the pursuit of greatness.

When we reached out to the remarkable men you will read about in the pages that follow, we discovered an other-worldly wisdom, a calm and confidence, a distinct sense of purpose and intent. Each of them granted us an interview because of their respect for Matt and their interest in contributing to this body of work. Jason Witten said it to me this way, "Matt was a great center, played a long time, and finished it up the right way. And along the way he managed to make a positive impact on a lot of lives by the way he conducted himself on a daily basis. That is true greatness, and that's the way I strive to be." Pretty cool coming from arguably the best tight end in the NFL.

I have known Matt for many years. Living next door to each other, we have spent many an afternoon out in the culdesac watching his tribe of six children, all under the age of eleven. Matt and I support each another in our respective life journeys, continually helping each other to stay the course and assisting others in doing likewise. Helping others - that is the inspiration for bringing you this book - to pass along some wise counsel. We call it All-Pro Wisdom.

I believe that each of us, at some level, want to achieve greatness. As I explored the inner life of these great men, I was encouraged. Why? Because it affirmed my conviction you and I can make the same choices, achieve personal greatness, and become a person of positive influence. The choices we are talking about are neither reserved for the elite and exceptionally gifted nor set apart for those who appear to have it all. They are for every person.

Over the years of my own development I have noticed a common set of attributes in the lives of my successful associates, and ultimately in many of those whom I have been privileged to lead. Not surprisingly, the traits of hard work, determination, perseverance, positive attitude, self-discipline, and a grateful spirit show up in the lives of exceptional achievers.

But some achievers seem to simply "lose their way". Without knowing it, they drift from their mission, or in some cases, have never understood or articulated their mission from the beginning. Like a meteor flashing through the night sky, they are brilliant for a period of time, and then vanish from sight.

People of greatness have staying power, combined with the right motivation and the right direction. They possess an internal engine guided by a dependable compass, and personal attributes directed by an orientation for excellence. Their trajectory is determined by a set of choices that are dependable, attainable, and sustainable.

Individuals and organizations; work associates and management teams; collegiate athletes and high school students; academic achievers and campus leaders; teachers and coaches; all ages and walks of life; female and male; all leaders setting their respective worlds on fire with clarity of purpose and intention. These "impact players" have grasped the Seven Choices, a common framework for developing disciplines and behaviors that inform and orient every aspect of their lives.

Perhaps you are looking to take your game to a new level, give your life a lift, or even create a fresh start. The Seven Choices you will be introduced to in this book can bring your spirit alive and create that spark of encouragement you may need to set your own life on a trajectory for greatness.

The Seven Choices are right in front of you. Right now. Personally accessible. Yours for the making. No matter your work environment, your boss, your coach, your family, or your life circumstance, there is no obstacle to prevent you from making the Seven Choices.

"Though no one can go back and make a brand new start, any one can start from now and make a brand new ending."
–CARL BARD, Scottish Writer

Greatness is within your grasp!

The choices are up to you.

Rich Chapman

January 2014

"Talent can get you to the NFL, but it won't keep you there. Football, like life, is a character game. It tests you and it pushes you. And it will reveal your true character."

MATT BIRK

THE CHOICES THAT SHAPE YOUR LIFE

I first went out for organized football in fourth grade. It was an intramural league, which was meant to be a way of introducing young, nice kids to the brutal world and culture of football. I was convinced I was a quarterback/running back/wide receiver hybrid. Certainly not a lineman. In my opinion, I could do it all. A tremendous talent on the brink of blossoming. I really wasn't aware, or maybe a better way to state it is it didn't really matter to me that I was a bit chubby as a kid. Fat, actually. The coaches took one look at me and said, "Lineman."

I can't remember if I enjoyed the experience that much or not. I do remember that it was pretty important to me and my group of friends that we played football. We thought it meant that we were tough, that we were men. It was a rite of passage. I guess that was a good enough reason for me to play the next year.

Heck, I played everything back then. I didn't need a reason, I loved sports. So, when the summer before fifth grade rolled around, I dug out my pads and helmet and bicycled up to the fields again.

It was the second evening of practice, and you didn't need to be a meteorologist to recognize that a storm was coming. The sky was black, scary black. All this seemed to be lost on our coaches—they kept blowing the whistles and yelling out instructions. I was with the other linemen, relegated to the far corner of the field, making sure we didn't get in the way of the "skill" players. Finally, as debris was getting blown up from the ground and raindrops began to pelt us, the coach called us up and told us to head home. Not a problem for most of the kids, whose parents had shown up to give them a ride home. It was a mad dash to the parking lot, like the way those people run in Spain when getting chased by the bulls. But it's a problem when your mom has the lone family car at work.

I do remember the bike ride home. It was only a few blocks, but it seemed like the Tour de France. I wore my helmet because branches were snapping and falling off trees all around me. It was like a mine field. It was raining so hard I could barely see. Fortunately, I had biked to the rec center about one million times in my life, so I probably could have done it with my eyes closed anyway. I arrived home, drenched and relieved. I walked in the door and my dad asked for an explanation as to what my football coach was thinking. I had no good answer.

My soccer career began the next day.

I picked up the game again in tenth grade. I lowered my sights to tight end, but on the first day of practice I was told I would be playing offensive line. It was like there was some powerful secret society at work, keeping the ball out of my hands at all costs. The football gods were still angry with me for quitting the sport in elementary school (a fact my friends loved to rib me about, and still do to this day). *"Fine,"* I said to myself. *"I'll play offensive line. I'll only be playing this silly sport for a year anyway. It's not like I'm going out for varsity after this. Those guys are huge. I'll get killed."*

I won't bore you with the rest of the details, but the essentials of the rest of the story go like this: I was coaxed into playing varsity, then thought I was done with football until I was recruited by Harvard. I thought, *"Yeah, why not?"* My senior year in Cambridge, Massachusetts, I had a financial analyst position locked up on Wall Street with Prudential Securities, but NFL scouts started showing up on campus. I was as curious about them as they were about me. I figured I would put the rest of my life on hold for a few months and go through the NFL experience. I can't remember what my expectations were, if any.

Being a long-shot, maybe I thought I would give it the old college try, get cut, and come out of it with a few great stories that I could tell over and over for the rest of my life. That would have been good enough for me. I wasn't supposed to make it. It was the NFL. We all know the odds. One in a million.

A Regular Guy

Now you know why I consider myself the most unlikely professional football player ever. For my entire NFL career, I felt like I was a participant in one of those fantasy camps, but mine lasted fifteen years. I was and still am a huge sports fan—a sports nut. I feel like somehow it links me to my childhood. I love talking sports strategies and philosophies, but what I love more is the human element. I look at myself as a very regular guy, but I have always been fascinated by greatness. Who isn't? For fifteen years my "office" was an NFL locker room. I got the up-close-and-personal look at the very best of the best. I was fascinated by these guys, who first were my idols on the Minnesota Vikings, including some of the guys I grew up rooting for when I was growing up in St. Paul, then teammates like Adrian Peterson, Jared Allen, Anquan Boldin and Joe Flacco.

Everyone knows *about* these guys, but I actually *know* these guys. I studied them. I ate meals with them. I trained with them. I sat in meetings with them. I rode on buses, flew on airplanes, stayed at hotels with them. And, most importantly, I got to put on the same uniform as them. I was honored to call these guys my teammates, and I was equally honored to play against some of the very best in football. Football players come in all shapes and sizes, races, religions, creeds, and parts of the world, but we are more alike than we are different. The NFL is a fraternity, and an exclusive one at that. The only other people who know what an NFL player goes through are other NFL players.

A Game of Character

I learned something very early in my career and it was confirmed every opportunity I had to play with a superstar: Talent can get you to the NFL, but it won't keep you there. I observed that football, like life, is a character game. Football is a game, but it is hard. It tests you, it pushes you. It is a labor of love. And it will develop and reveal your true character.

I wasn't a big-name talent, but like those aforementioned superstars and others interviewed for this book, I accomplished many things during my career. I believe deep in my heart and my gut that we succeeded because we played the character game as well as the game on the field.

Looking back, fifteen years is a long run in a pro game, given all of its inherent uncertainties. And I enjoyed myself for every minute of that run, since I never expected to make it at all. I can honestly say that it never got old going to work at the stadium or practice facility. Every day, when I got to the entrance I had my little moment, saying to myself, *"I can't believe this is where I work!"*

Winning the 2013 Super Bowl 34-31 in one of the most exciting nail-biters in Super Bowl history was almost too good to be true. We made the big plays and, even with the 49ers' feverish comeback after the lights went out in the Mercedes-Benz Superdome, we kept our focus.

MATT BIRK

"My best memory was seeing my family and friends flood onto the field. It was truly an 'I can't believe this is happening' moment, where words were replaced by laughter. It is nearly impossible to find any words that can define an experience like that."

More importantly, however, win or lose, I was able to come away from the Super Bowl convinced that I had achieved what I wanted to, that I was in a place that I had worked so long and so hard to reach.

My best memory of the post-game celebration was seeing my family and friends flood onto the field. Holding the Lombardi trophy was cool, I guess, but experiencing something like that with the ones that mean the most to you, now that's powerful. It was one of those "I can't believe this is happening" moments, where words were replaced by laughter. Who would be dumb enough to try to explain or define a moment like that?

My pre- and post-game reflections led me to contemplate the principles and choices that drove me, as a man, toward a fuller life. That is the journey I refer to, a constant search for the truth. My journey in the NFL was one of great growth—personally, spiritually, professionally. It was a continual learning process, and along the way I learned some fairly basic principles, ones that I was eager to set down in print for others to benefit from, not as a guru but hopefully as an example.

Alas, this book is not about me or football. Guys that succeed on NFL football fields do so because of the men they are off the field, as well as who they are one on the field. From the first day of my career, I was in awe of so many of my teammates. Some of these guys could have been successful doing anything, but their main talent was football. There is no downside to standing shoulder-to-shoulder with these types of people on a daily basis. I am a better man for being around the players and coaches I had the privilege to play with and for. I really miss those guys. I learned a lot from them and from the game. That's what this book is about.

My Inspirations

The insights and lessons I will be sharing with you in this book come from three major sources:

First, are the great players and coaches I had the privilege of working with during my fifteen years in the NFL. Players and coaches come and go, but I found that the truly great ones who had real staying power were very intentional about the choices they made in their lives.

Second, many of the insights I will be sharing with you come from the notebooks I kept over the years. I have always been a student of life, and whenever I come across fascinating lessons or quotations, I write them down in my notebooks. Many of these insights come from ball players, but others come from business tycoons, novels I read, movies I see, or even the homilies I hear on Sunday mornings.

And third, is my friend and mentor Rich Chapman. Rich is a successful business and community leader who was my next-door neighbor for the decade I lived in Minnesota. Over the years as Rich and I got to know each other, we discovered that we shared the same values, convictions and faith.

Rich helped me organize all the ideas I had been collecting in my notebooks and frame them into the Seven Choices. Rich is no stranger to sports, being an NCAA All-American basketball player. That, in addition to his years of leadership experience, made our collaboration very natural and energizing. There would be no book without Rich, and I'm grateful that he challenged me, encouraged me, and collaborated with me on this project.

One thing I found inspiring was that faith plays a leading role to each of the men we interviewed. It showed that for many of us who strive for excellence through self-understanding, God is alive and well. That was nice to know. Anquan Boldin may have said it best: "I know what I'm here for on this Earth." Once we know that, we have a much better chance of making the right choices.

CHAPTER ONE

WHO ARE YOU?

"BE YOURSELF. EVERYONE ELSE IS ALREADY TAKEN."

—OSCAR WILDE

CHOOSE TO UNDERSTAND YOUR IDENTITY

I had always felt there was much more to life than football. I didn't grow up playing the game, and I never really saw myself as a football player. In high school, I enjoyed many other interests. I played the villain in the musical "Hurricane Smith," went on a mission trip to Guatemala my senior year, enjoyed reading serious books, and took honors classes. I was all over the place in my activities and interests, not just a "jock."

Then a strange thing happened as my football career evolved. When you play in the NFL, people always want to talk to you about football, football, football. In their mind, they identified me with football. That's it. It's like I was incapable of talking about anything else.

But that wasn't how I saw things. I was always very careful to make sure I didn't let football become my entire identity. My confidence to be myself came from an understanding that *football was not who I was, it was something that I did.*

Identity is a tricky thing. For many people, it is wrapped up with their work or career. For others, identity is connected to their accomplishments in life, or the homes and cars and possessions they have acquired. Then again, identity can often be about dreams for the future and the goals we have for ourselves.

Everyone seems to have a different approach to finding

and living out their identity. And if there's one thing I have learned, it's that identity is not something that is given to you at birth. Rather, identity is a choice. It comes down to the things you value and the choices you make. What about you?

Do you have enough confidence to always be yourself, or do you find yourself letting others define who you are?

It's a scary question if you haven't given much thought to it. If you haven't been cognizant of what your choices say about you and what you are about, this might be the scariest question in the world, but it's one that needs to be asked.

Chance or Choice?

You will either establish your own identity, or someone else will do it for you. My main goal in this chapter is to persuade you to understand that you have more influence on who you are than anybody else.

You don't get to choose who your parents are, where you were born, your race, or your DNA. There are many, many choices you don't get to make. But even though these important life choices were determined by others, the biggest choices in life are still up to you.

That's because you do get to choose who you will be. No one else can determine your identity, unless you let them. It's your choices that both reflect and shape who you are.

How can other people shape your identity? It's easy. If you are not sure who you are, you can be swayed by friends. You can be controlled by people's criticism and judgments. You can try to be a people pleaser, living in anxiety and fear of offending others, or failing to meet their expectations. In other words, you just go along with the crowd and popular opinion.

Even advertising can shape us. We live in a world of endless stimuli and distraction.

We are exposed to millions of hours of ads telling us that we will be sexy, popular, smart, hip and cool if only we buy the right products. This can have a powerful influence on how people spend their money, how they see themselves, and, ultimately, what they value.

Being yourself may seem like something that's easy and natural, but it's actually a full-time job that you need to work on with intentionality. It can't be something that you ignore or leave to others.

George Bernard Shaw said, "Life is not about finding yourself. It's about creating yourself."

I learned that the hard way during my rookie season. To my surprise, I had been drafted by the Minnesota Vikings. Soon, I was working as hard as I could during our spring minicamps.

One night after practice I was sitting in a hotel room and thought I would skim through a sports magazine when I came across an article evaluating all the NFL's rookies. Excitedly, I turned the pages until I came to the evaluation of me. My excitement quickly turned to anger and frustration.

The article was based on the prognostications of Mel Kiper, perhaps the best-known "draft guru." Unfortunately, he didn't have much good to say about me.

In the article, Kiper said I wasn't strong enough or fast enough to make it in the NFL. He predicted I wouldn't be around long as a Viking, unless I learned how to be a long snapper.

My reaction to these negative predictions was intense. First, I was embarrassed. Everyone is going to read these unflattering things about me. Next, I was questioning why I was even trying to make the team. I started thinking maybe this whole thing about trying to make it in the NFL was an exercise in futility. My emotions were going pretty crazy, all this in the span of about ten seconds. But then I caught myself and I said aloud to nobody in particular:

"Who the heck is Mel Kiper?

"How can this one guy tell the world how all the NFL rookies will play this season? None of these players have yet played a single down!

"And who is he to tell me what kind of player I am going to be (or not going to be)?"

Kiper's pessimistic predictions about each new crop of NFL rookies were merely one of the many things that make some NFL players wonder about their abilities and question who they really are.

It seems like the entire system of the NFL, and life for that matter, is set up from day one to challenge you, frustrate you, and test you. You must prove yourself to be worthy. Like it or not, that's the way it is. There is constant evaluation, criticism, and pressure to improve. And particularly for young players, and young people, you are constantly striving to gain the approval of others, which is a dangerous thing in and of itself.

Every year, I saw many young, talented and confident players come into the league. None of us had any idea what we were getting ourselves into. In time, many began to doubt themselves and question who they were. It can become a real slippery slope.

Thankfully, I have always been blessed with a good measure of self-identity and, therefore, self-confidence. As a result, other peoples' opinions of me have never mattered that much to me, one way or the other. I have found this to be a great source of strength to me, even a weapon during tough times.

Learn Who You Are

The boy was seven years old, but he didn't talk much. Instead, he often mumbled sentences to himself, a behavior that led others to assume that he was not too bright.

Later, some of his teachers thought he had learning disabilities because he was not very good at memorizing facts and details. Later still, he flunked the entrance exam for the college he hoped to attend.

His name was Albert Einstein.

Another boy was put up for adoption right after he was born. His adoptive parents promised to encourage him to attend college, but he flunked out after six months. He survived by begging his friends to let him sleep on their floors and turning in pop bottles for food money.

His name was Steve Jobs, founder of Apple. Nobody would have ever heard of Einstein or Jobs if these two men had continued to fail in school and in life. But as we know, they chose to ignore the rejection and assessments of others and learn to be who they were created to be.

Finally, my favorite. There was a boy born into poverty who had political aspirations. He was a voracious reader and became very well educated.

But he was not very good at winning elections. He lost eight of them in total, including two bids for U.S. Congress and two bids for U.S. Senate. But he won the big one! He became our 16th President, and one of the greatest leaders in the history of the United States.

His name was Abraham Lincoln.

Perhaps you have grown up facing difficult circumstances, or hearing other people predict that you will be a failure. Perhaps you have even had people scoff at your dreams, or remind you of your shortcomings. Join the club—the not-so-exclusive club. Sometimes we think our problems are unique to us, but what we go through has been endured and conquered over and over throughout history.

I am here to tell you that others don't get to determine who you are unless you let them. That is up to you.

You may be thinking, *"So how do I choose to understand*

MY identity?" Try this: Consider what you are about, what you want to be about, and what you want to stand for? what the ideal you would look like. *Is that the person you see when you look in the mirror?*

I was wrapping up my senior year of college, and even though playing football was my dream, I knew I had to be practical and line up a Plan B just in case. That's what took me to Wall Street and a planned job at one of the nation's big investment firms.

But when I told my boss about my aspirations to play in the NFL he was a bit surprised.

"Really? You think you might actually make it in the NFL?" he asked.

I didn't let it get me down or kill my dreams because I knew who I was and I knew what was important to me. I didn't know if I would succeed or fail in my quest to make it in the NFL, but I was going to chase my dream. That's what mattered to me. *Because my*

identity was secure, I had the confidence to be myself and to live my own life. People could discount or dismiss me, but it didn't change the reality of who I was.

As you may know, Dallas Cowboy and All-Pro tight end Jason Witten was removed from his family of origin at a young age due to domestic violence. He is known around the league as a class act. I got the opportunity to play with Jason in a couple of Pro Bowls, and I discovered that he is better than advertised, both as a player and as a person. When all is all said and done, he will go down as one of the greatest, if not the greatest tight end in the history of the NFL.

Jason says it like this:

"Identity starts with inner strength. Knowing who you are and who you serve. Everything else feeds off of that."
–JASON WITTEN

When critics told me I was

... others don't get to determine who you are unless you let them.

"Identity starts with inner strength. Knowing who you are and who you serve. Everything else feeds off of that."

JASON WITTEN

too weak to play in the NFL, I said "OK." I decided that I was going to make myself tougher than my competition. I dedicated myself to the weight room. I also developed the conviction that, *"When it is too tough for everyone else, it is just right for me."*

You can either choose your identity, or someone will do it for you.

Becoming the Ideal You

If you don't know who you are, critics can shake you up and confuse you about your identity. So can circumstances. Just ask Aaron Rodgers.

Aaron was 5' 10" tall and weighed only 165 pounds when soaking wet, but he confounded skeptics to become a star quarterback at the University of California, Berkeley, where he broke a number of passing records.

Widely predicted to be the first or second overall selection leading up to the 2005 NFL Draft, it was astonishing to watch Aaron slide down the draft boards, until he landed with the Green Bay Packers as the twenty-fifth pick.

The only thing was, the Packers already had a quarterback. You may have heard of him—Brett Favre.

Apparently, the so-called "experts" didn't think too highly of Aaron's talents, or that, at the very least, he was over-hyped and overrated. Aaron sat on the bench much of his first three seasons. Being on the bench is difficult. But Aaron didn't let circumstances get him down. Instead, he continued working hard on his technique and skills. When opportunity knocked, he was ready.

He became the Packers' starting quarterback in 2008, and you know the rest of the story. He led his team to victory in the Super Bowl after the 2010 season, and was named the Super Bowl MVP.

Plus, all the work he did

"I like to be consistent. That is a good word for me. It is being the kind of person that I'd like to be every single day. When I'm at the stadium, it's being the kind of teammate I want to be, the kind of man I want to be, and to choose what I want to stand for."

AARON RODGERS

behind the scenes during his years on the bench has enabled him to set the record for the highest career passer rating in NFL history, a rating higher than Steve Young's, Tom Brady's, or Peyton Manning's.

To me, Aaron is a great example of somebody who is comfortable in his own skin. He is successful, respected and skillful, but at the same time, he is relaxed and puts others at ease.

"I like to be consistent. That is a good word for me. It is being the kind of person that I'd like to be every single day. First and foremost, that is my attitude when I wake up in the morning looking at the day as an opportunity to remember what kind of person I want to be. When I'm at the stadium, it's being the kind of teammate I want to be, the kind of man I want to be, and to choose what I want to stand for."
–AARON RODGERS

It's the work you do on your own, in private and out of the spotlight that contributes to forming your identity. It's not the freaky or accidental things. It's not the fabulous or the horrible things. It's the choices you make day after day that will reflect who you really are.

In the words of St. Francis de Sales: "Be who you are and be that well."

Be Intentional, Not Accidental

One of my primary life principles is intentionality. In other words, put some thought into what you are doing and why you are doing it. Don't just go through the motions mindlessly. Be intentional about what you're doing. Identity definitely falls into that category.

Unfortunately, some people don't seem to realize that their identity is something that they can control and develop. They can become passive, allowing other people and forces to shape who they are and their beliefs and values. *Why would you let someone else decide something of such significance?*

For example, my identity as a center was created very intentionally through thousands of hours of practice. I worked to develop my skills. I learned my strengths and weaknesses. I didn't go onto the field on game day and try to figure out my game. I knew who I was as a player. Understanding that gave me confidence, and the best chance for success.

Coach John Harbaugh puts it this way:

> **"Identity is shown by not just talking about it, but by what I do every single day. It's doing my best regardless of the circumstance. It's making the right decisions over and over and over again. Being great today."**
> **–JOHN HARBAUGH**

Being intentional about your identity is as important for teams as it is for individuals. When I became a free agent in 2009, I was invited by Coach John Harbaugh to come to Baltimore for a meeting. He had just finished his first year as a head coach in the NFL. Within thirty minutes, I knew this was where I wanted to be. Why? Coach Harbaugh clearly articulated the identity of the Ravens. He told me, "No matter what, we are going to work really hard and get as good as we can get. Tough and physical football is what we are about. Regardless of wins and losses, we know what we stand for."

During the season, teams win and teams lose. Nobody likes losing, but teams that know who they are don't let losses confuse them about their team's identity. Win or lose, you need to be who you are. You work hard to do better day by day, but you don't try to turn your team into something it is not. You stay with who you are.

Identity Foreclosure

After the Ravens' Super Bowl victory in February of 2013, I retired from the NFL. This change was difficult after so many years, but the decision to retire allowed me to practice what I preach. I always say that my identity is not completely wrapped up in football. Here was my chance to focus time and energy on the rest of my life.

This is harder than it sounds

JOHN HARBAUGH

"Identity is shown by not just talking about it, but by what I do every single day. It's doing my best regardless of the circumstance. It's making the right decisions over and over and over again. Being great today."

"Football is what I do. It does not define who I am. God, husband, father, son of my parents, football. In that order."

JARED ALLEN

for some players who have only known football, football, football since they were nine or ten years old. Yes, many NFL football players do struggle when their playing days are over, and this is because they have not been thoughtful about choosing to establish their *own* identity. Many NFLers, from a pre-teen age, were recognized for being athletically gifted. This is very common for many boys and young men. Our culture places a heightened emphasis on sports. As these "stars" go through high school, they are showered with adulation. Big-time college football does little to encourage these young men to think about anything outside of what's going on in the stadium on Saturday afternoon. Some of them make it to the NFL, thinking the ride will never end. Football is such a huge part of these guys' lives and their public persona that they suffer from what experts refer to as "identity foreclosure."

In essence, at a young age,

these guys stopped growing and settled on football as their identity. Everything about them was wrapped up in the game. I am sure you can think of some examples of what I am talking about. They never made the choice to be who they were meant to be, they let everybody else choose for them. This happens not only to professional football players, it happens in all walks of life.

Jared Allen, All-Pro defensive end of the Minnesota Vikings, sums it up perfectly:

> **"Football is what I do. It does not define who I am. God, husband, father, son of my parents, football. In that order."**
> **—JARED ALLEN**

The circumstances of your life will continuously change from day to day. You may live in different countries, work for different companies, and hang out with different people.

If you know who you are deep inside, you will have a rooted sense of identity that carries you through all the changes you face, the rest of your life will be easier and happier, and you will have a more positive impact on the people you influence.

Our identity must be certain. It is at the core of all our relationships, family, activities, and challenges. When our self-concept and fundamental identity is clearly understood, we will be secure and confident in the choices we make.

WHAT'S THE PAYOFF?

Choosing to understand my IDENTITY gives me the CONFIDENCE to be myself.

CHAPTER TWO

WHAT IS YOUR PURPOSE?

"A MAN WITHOUT A PURPOSE IS LIKE A SHIP
WITHOUT A RUDDER; A WAIF, A NOTHING, A NO MAN."

–THOMAS CARLYLE

CHOOSE TO DISCOVER YOUR MISSION

Most everyone has those days where they have second thoughts and question the purpose of what they are doing.

I certainly questioned my purpose for playing football the day I returned to my home turf of Minnesota as a member of the Baltimore Ravens. I had played for the Vikings for more than a decade. Now I had swapped purples, and was standing once again on the field I knew so well. But this time, I was standing on the visitors' sideline of the HHH Metrodome.

The Ravens were under pressure to perform. We were 3-2, having lost our last two games, while the Vikings were 5-0 and riding high with a new quarterback with an unusual name: Favre. For me, this game was an opportunity to show my hometown fans that I had made the right decision to switch teams. Needless to say, I was jacked up and ready to go. The second play of the game, we ran the ball up the middle and E.J. Henderson, middle linebacker for the Vikes and my teammate for many years, came downhill and we collided. E.J. was a hitter. As they say, he could "bring the wood."

In a split second, an intense pain shot down my shoulder. It was a neck stinger, something that was not foreign to me. A neck stinger is when the nerve gets pinched or irritated. Fortunately, this was an old, recurring injury and I knew I was not at any risk for long-term damage. Unfortunately, it hurt like hell. I remember thinking, *"Great. Only sixty-five more plays to go!"*

At moments like this, I would often ask myself questions like:

"Is it worth it to do this?"

"Is this what I'm supposed to be doing with my body?"

There were other times when the questions I asked myself went even deeper, touching on those fundamental, foundational questions that each and every one of us ask ourselves from time to time, like:

"Is this what I was placed here on this Earth to do?"

We don't always like to ask ourselves this kind of question, but it is one of the most important things we can ask. Sometimes questions like this sneak up on us, rising up from our subconscious and confronting us at the most unexpected times. Maybe we fear what the answer may be?

Some people never seem to think about their purpose in life. And many people who do get frustrated because the road of life is not marked with bright neon lights or clear directional signals that tell them which way to turn or what path to take.

What about you? Have you ever asked yourself what your purpose is in life? I hope you have, because I am convinced that if you regularly ask yourself this difficult question, you will ultimately learn more about what your purpose truly is and bring deeper meaning to each area of your life.

Do you have a mission that gives meaning to all of your pursuits, or are you uncertain about why you do the things you do?

Defining Success

In the movie, *As Good as It Gets*, Jack Nicholson plays a successful writer who struggles with a number of deep personal issues. No matter how successful he becomes, he is not happy, even though he has achieved and amassed most of the things that our culture places emphasis on. This leads him to ask a question that most of us ask from time to time:

"Is this as good as it gets?"

Sometimes people answer this question with a definite no. "There's got to be more to life than this," they say.

Part of the problem may be the way they define success. I know some people who measure their lives based on a short list of things they think they need to achieve true happiness:

Prestigious job with a big paycheck?

Comfortable house in the suburbs?

Nice car with all the gadgets?

Six pack abs?

"It all goes deeper than what you see on the surface. I know that everything I have comes from God above."
—ADRIAN PETERSON

But life has a way of shaking people up, making them question their checklists. Coach Harbaugh is a man who is open to new ways of thinking, and is very innovative. It is always clear to those around him that he has a sense of purpose and intention.

"If I want to create my own path, the possibilities become very limiting. The possibilities God has for us are enormous and fabulous. Why be limited by yourself, by your own thoughts? I let God determine what my mission is. The possibilities are limitless with God."
—JOHN HARBAUGH

If you are intentional and even relentless about finding your purpose and pursuing it with all of your heart, your mission in life will become clear to you.

Bigger than Big?

Everything about professional football shouts BIG!

The players are big.
The salaries are big.
The stadiums where we play are big.

And the revenues are big, including the cost of fans' season tickets, the billion dollar television rights the

ADRIAN PETERSON

"It all goes deeper than what you see on the surface. I know that everything I have comes from God above."

"My purpose is definitely a lot bigger than playing football." ←

JASON WITTEN

networks buy up, and the advertising rates the networks charge companies to run their commercials. (A 30-second commercial during the 2013 Super Bowl, for example, cost a record $4 million.)

When you are in the middle of all this activity, you experience all this bigness every day. There is an undeniable aura and mystique to playing in the NFL that gives the whole scene an energetic glow.

> **"My purpose is definitely a lot bigger than playing football."**
> **–JASON WITTEN**

Every week in practice, Sunday's upcoming game is the biggest event on the horizon. But then a funny thing happens. Once Sunday's game is over and the game statistics are tallied, this once-big game suddenly seems like ancient history. Now, it's next Sunday's game that is the big event of the future.

After every game, I'd be in front of my locker still dressed in half of my uniform, and some media members would walk up and ask me about our next game. I felt like saying, "Wait a minute! I haven't even washed the stink off me from this game, and you're already asking about the next one?"

The same thing happens with the Super Bowl. Playing in one is awesome. Winning the big game is even better. But let me ask you a question: "Can you tell me who won the Super Bowl three years ago?"

Most people don't have a clue. Over time, something that was very, very big now looks smaller and less significant.

It's like Marv Levy, the Pro Football Hall of Fame coach for the Kansas City Chiefs and the Buffalo Bills, once said. A reporter asked Levy if the next game was a must-win game.

"This is not a must-win," said Coach Levy. "World War II was a must-win."

In other words, next week's game ain't life or death. And what's true in football is true in other areas of life, too.

"This is not a must-win," said Coach Levy. "World War II was a must-win."

Troy Polamalu rarely gives an interview. But he wanted to help us with this book in explaining his view on important choices and seeking a purpose in life. Troy is one of the most prolific strong safeties in the NFL. He brings it every game, and is a fierce competitor. You can truly say there has never been a player like Troy. Flat out, he is a playmaker. Each time we played the Steelers, our offensive gameplan started with "finding #43." We had to account for him at all times. It's like he invented ways to make plays from the safety position. He is regarded by many as the best safety to ever play the game.

Each time we played the Steelers, I wondered if I would be faced with trying to block him. That's the kind of respect he gets around the league. Troy is a game changer. Beneath his football persona and fiery style of play, however, lies a family man of deep compassion, intention, and purpose.

"If I could articulate my purpose within my life, it is just to be available for God to use. As a by-product of that, I will be a great husband to my wife, a great father to my children. Everything else in life will fall in place." –TROY POLAMALU

Some people think their next car or iPhone model will change their lives. But a few days after the purchase has been made, the car has been driven around town, and the phone's new gadgets aren't so new anymore, and people realize there's nothing that big about buying more stuff.

Has this has ever happened to you? You set your heart on the next big thing, only to discover once you achieve your goal that it's not so big a thing after all. If this pattern seems familiar, you face an important choice. Are you now going to set your mind on the next big thing that probably won't be that big? Or are you going to focus instead on something even bigger, something deeper?

Your questions about purpose in life force you to look at life with a wiser perspective. Instead of going for the next big thing, or being blown about by whatever wind is moving today, finding your purpose gives you a foundation. It gives you passion, which fuels your ambitions so you can reach out and impact the world.

TROY POLAMALU

"If I could articulate my purpose within my life, it is just to be available for God to use. As a byproduct of that, I will be a great husband to my wife, a great father to my children. Everything else in life will fall in place."

Going Beyond Self

During my rookie year with the Vikings, I reached out to others through something called Community Tuesday. Players practiced on Monday, but were given Tuesdays off. Our coach, Denny Green, encouraged us to do something for the community on those days off.

I was new to the team, and quite grateful to have a spot on the roster, so if Coach Green suggested we get out and do something in the community, he didn't have to tell me twice. I went straight to Brad Madson, community relations director for the team, and asked him to use me how he saw fit.

The next morning I found myself at an inner city school that was in a part of Minneapolis I had never known existed before, even though I had grown up in the Twin Cities.

Because I was a brand new and unknown member of the Vikings, I assumed nobody would care about me being at the school. As soon as the principal introduced me to the students, they went completely bananas.

I talked to the students about something that really matters to me: getting a good education.

"All of you can see that I am a football player right now," I said. "But the thing I'm proudest about in my life isn't being on this team. The thing I'm proudest about is having a good education.

"If I live until I am 100 years old, my education will serve me much longer than my experience in the NFL will. So, I want to ask you today, will you promise me to stay in school and get a good education? Raise your hands if you promise to do that."

A zillion hands flew up into the air.

Being with these kids was such a rush that I made a habit to go to as many schools as I could on Community Tuesdays. I was passionate about talking to kids and encouraging them to study and stay in school. I still believe in that with all my heart.

Deciding to Make a Difference

But over time, I wondered if my little talks with students were making any difference in their lives. Sure, it was exciting to go to schools for one-time events, but I wanted to do something that had staying power. If possible, I wanted to change some kids' lives for the long haul.

I sat down with my wife, Adrianna, and she helped me think more strategically. That was when I started the HIKE Foundation. The name stands for Hope, Inspiration, Knowledge, and Education.

I created HIKE to support reading programs in schools because I knew that if kids can't read, they can't study, they can't get good grades, they can't graduate. But if they learn to read, they can pursue these goals. Reading is the foundation of every child's education.

The more time and energy I invested in HIKE, the more excited I became about encouraging kids to pursue their dreams. My purpose in life was coming into clearer focus. And when I moved to Baltimore to play for the Ravens, I took HIKE with me so I could impact schools there, too.

Many of the men and women I respect most and who have the strongest sense of purpose in their lives have learned this very important lesson about going beyond themselves. Instead of remaining wrapped up in their own lives and their own narrow concerns, they give themselves to others in a spirit of humility and service.

"The moment when problems spring up on you that you weren't anticipating and you have the chance for interaction with someone, you just decide to drop everything and make the time for it. This is your

opportunity for your finest hour. Your finest moment. Your eternal moment."
–JOHN HARBAUGH

Even with my limited amount of charitable work, I can tell you that reaching out and serving others is something that gives my life meaning and purpose.

Are you doing anything to go beyond yourself and reach out to others? If you want to find out what your purpose is, I encourage you to open your mind and your heart and try doing something good for someone else. This will be a rewarding experience both for you and the people who receive your help. The late John Wooden, who gets my vote

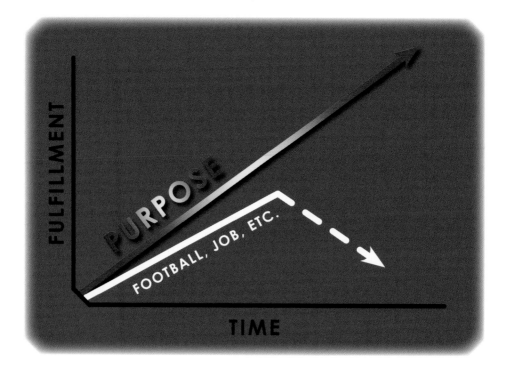

"YOUR PURPOSE" WILL GROW AND LAST FOR YOUR ENTIRE LIFE. ACCOMPLISHMENTS ARE FLEETING.

for the greatest coach of all time, said this: "You can't have a perfect day without doing something for someone who will never be able to repay you."

Many great NFL players are involved in charitable work. They don't always talk publicly about it, but they do it quietly and out of the spotlight.

Start Where You Are

Sometimes when I tell people about the HIKE charity, they reply by saying something like this: "I think your good work is great, and if I was as famous or as wealthy as you, I would do exactly the same thing!"

At that point I say: "Hold it right there!"

No matter who you are, what you do, how much money you have, where you live, or how famous you are (or aren't), you can start serving others today. You don't need to wait until you become wealthy or famous to help someone out. Wayne Kostroski a friend of

mine and founder of Taste of the NFL, likes to say "Give as you go." You can begin today by loving the people who are closest to you and reaching out to others you can touch.

Here's an experience that happened to me:

I was leaving the gym after working out one day when I saw a woman in the parking lot. She worked out at the same gym, so we knew each other a little bit.

"I hate to bother you, but I am here and my son is in the car. He gets picked on a lot at school because he's a little nerdy. Could you just come and say hello to him? It would mean a lot to him."

Just like you, I had places to go, things to do, people to see, right? But deep inside, I could hear a voice telling me, "Go see the kid!!!!"

I did go say hello to him, and I gave him an autograph. He seemed pretty darn happy. The next day, I ran into the mother again.

"Give as you go."
—WAYNE KOSTROSKI, founder, Taste of the NFL

She handed me a thank you card and she told me that she really appreciated me taking the time with her son. I still have that card today, and here is what it says:

"One hundred years from now, it will not matter what my bank account was, what house I lived in, or what car I drove. But the world may be different because I made a difference in the life of a child."

This mother wanted me to talk to her son because she thought an NFL player could give him hope and encouragement. Perhaps you are reading this book to read about All-Pros of the NFL. But know this: my purpose is no greater than yours. We simply have different platforms.

Through the years, I have met teachers, doctors, nurses, youth center directors, shelter directors, and all kinds of people who are making a difference on a daily basis. These people are changing lives.

You don't need to be an NFL star to do something for others. You can get started now by getting involved in the Boys and Girls Clubs of America in your local area. You can mentor a young student, coach a school basketball team, or volunteer to help underachieving students work on their reading or their math homework.

Maybe you think you don't have much to give to others. But if you have a desire to love others, you will discover that you have much to offer. And I believe that as you choose to step out of your personal comfort zone and seek to serve others, you will find your purpose.

Each of us needs a reason to live—a driving passion or calling that provides meaning and impact. This is a person's mission. Everything else in our life should contribute to this mission.

WHAT'S THE PAYOFF?

Choosing to live with PURPOSE gives me a MISSION to give meaning to all of my pursuits.

CHAPTER THREE

WHAT KIND OF PERSON DO YOU WANT TO BE?

"A LIFE OF REMARKABLE CHARACTER IS TO BE
PREFERRED OVER A LIFE OF REMARKABLE ACHIEVEMENT."

—FATHER FRANCIS FERNANDEZ

CHOOSE TO DEVELOP YOUR CHARACTER

It was a typical New England December night and we were playing in Foxboro Stadium for the 2011 AFC Championship. The New England Patriots had become one of our fiercest rivals. They had the allure of being the "pretty" team with the All-American boy Tom Brady playing quarterback and three Super Bowl wins on his resume. We were the team that nobody really wanted to see. The Baltimore Ravens were the opposite of pretty—we were a rough and tumble bunch who prided ourselves on leaving our opponents sore the next day. We played good, solid defense and tried to establish the running game—not exactly a brand of football that appealed to a lot of people. Nonetheless, this was the AFC Championship and we were sixty minutes away from our goal: the Super Bowl.

The game itself was as intense as any I had ever been in, but then again, it's supposed to be. I had to battle Vince Wilfork, New England's All-Pro nose tackle, for most of the game. Vince is as physically dominating of a player as there is in the NFL, and he was bringing it that day. He was having his way with me, but somehow late in the fourth quarter, we were only trailing by three, 23-20. We took the field with two minutes left in the game, convinced that if we gave the ball back to Brady and company, the game would be over.

Nothing came easy for us offensively on this day. But then things just started clicking. We began to methodically move the ball down the field, staying on schedule with the down and distance. We were marching our way destined to score, win this game, and go to the Super Bowl. I could feel it.

Inside of a minute, we were deep in Patriots' territory. Joe Flacco threw a perfect pass to Lee Evans in the back of the endzone, where Lee had it for a split second before Sterling Moore made a tremendous play knocking the ball out of his hands. For the nanosecond that Lee had the ball, it was amazing how many thoughts filled my head. For a brief moment, I was planning my trip to Indianapolis for the next game.

"No worries," I thought. Our sure-footed kicker Billy Cundiff trotted out onto the field with eleven seconds left in regulation to attempt a 32-yard field goal and send the game into overtime. We had

the momentum on our side big time. I still KNEW we were going to win.

But then the unthinkable happened. We missed the kick. The Patriots took a final knee and the game was officially over. Confetti was raining down on Foxboro and like a fighter who had just gotten knocked out cold, I didn't know what was going on.

And neither did anybody else in the locker room. The mood was more of astonishment than disappointment. We had been close for more than a few years. Many of the experts felt like we were not capable of breaking through and taking that "next step" as a football team. We felt like we had what it took, but each year, we were coming up short. I remember being numb in the locker room.

I started to "come to" on the long bus ride from Foxboro Stadium to Providence Airport. The bus was quiet, as you might expect, and the mood was quite reflective. I had not played well, and as much as missing out on a chance to go to the Super Bowl hurt, feeling like I had let my team down was eating me up on the inside.

As fate would have it, a year later we earned a trip back to Foxboro, again for the AFC Championship. But this time the outcome was different. It was as satisfying and as gratifying a victory as I had ever been a part of, but not just because we advanced to the Super Bowl. While going back there a year later and winning may have proven that were a good football team capable of winning big games, what it really showed was that we had character, the stuff that champions are made of. The loss the previous year was as excruciating as any I had ever experienced, but we kept our chins up and our chests out.

Two weeks later, confetti was raining down again, but this time in the middle of the Superdome. My kids and I were rolling around in it like pigs in mud. I looked up on the

scoreboard and it said, "The Baltimore Ravens are Super Bowl XLVII Champions." To me, in words not seen, the scoreboard message was saying, "The Baltimore Ravens are a Team of Character."

Do you have the charater you need to perform with consistency, or do you find yourself being blown about by the surface winds of life?

Contents under Pressure

You often hear people talk about the importance of character, but it seems many of us aren't really sure what character is, or where it comes from.

Many people seem to believe that character is something you're born with, like your last name. But I have good news for you. Character is like the other topics we are exploring in this book. It's a choice you make. Or, more precisely, character is the result of the millions of choices you make throughout your life.

Following our loss to the Patriots, we as a team could have easily made a series of bad choices. We could have blamed one another for the loss. This could have done irreparable harm to our team chemistry. We could have felt sorry for ourselves, gone out and behaved foolishly, irresponsibly. More than one NFL career has ended because of one night out and a few bad decisions. We could have ended up losing a lot more than just the game. For example, I wanted to activate the dental plan of the sportswriter who asked me if I realized that back in 1998, my rookie season with the Minnesota Vikings had ended a similar way when our place kicker Gary Anderson, who had not missed a field goal or extra point all season, missed what would have been the game-clinching field goal in our NFC Championship game against Atlanta.

"No, I didn't realize that. But thanks for asking!"

Instead of choosing these or many other bad options, we were determined to stand firm, learn what we could from our loss, and make the most of whatever opportunities life would bring us next.

Some people say that football builds character, and I believe that it can. Things happen and you choose how to respond. It's equally true that football reveals your character. If you have given it some thought before the moments of truth arrive, your actions will demonstrate if your character is deep-rooted in rock-solid principles, or if it is based on emotion you are feeling at a given time.

Life, just like football, builds and reveals your character.

It's like numerous parents and teachers repeatedly told me while I was growing up: "Character is who you are when nobody else is watching."

"Now that I am even in a greater leadership role,

Character is the result of the millions of choices you make throughout your life.

"Now that I am even in a greater leadership role, other guys are looking at me and looking at my charac-ter, looking at the way I talk. I want to be known as a good teammate who did what he said he was going to do and cares about other people and made them feel important."

AARON RODGERS

other guys are looking at me and looking at my character, looking at the way I talk. All this is important to me and I hope it registers with them. I want to be known as a good teammate who did what he said he was going to do and cares about other people and made them feel important. Hopefully, people will talk as much about that as what I accomplish on the field."
–AARON RODGERS

What about you? What do you do when you are under pressure? How do you respond when your dreams suddenly turn to dust? How do you treat family, friends, loved ones, co-workers, or your boss when your world goes upside down? It doesn't take too much effort to be an all-around great guy or girl when things are breaking your way. But the thing about life is this: The lows are guaranteed, the highs are not. That is a truth we need to prepare for and be ready to handle.

> *The decisions you make and the actions you display under pressure will reveal your true character.*

We should start getting ready. Today.

"Adversity has a way of introducing you to yourself. When you have to stand alone in making a decision, you discover the depth of your character."
–ROGER GOODELL

Chutes and Boards

If you've played team sports, you've probably heard coaches tell players to focus on the fundamentals. Coaches want consistency. They want players who are dependable, play after play, game after game. Coaches don't want players who are brilliant one moment and boneheaded the next. The way you develop consistency is by developing your foundation, which is built on the fundamentals.

In fact, just about everything people do in this world

involves fundamental skills that must be mastered.

If you master the fundamentals, you have a chance to achieve greatness. If you don't, you are destined for mediocrity.

If you want to be a successful lineman in the NFL, you need to master this fundamental: getting low and gaining leverage. That's because in the trenches, everybody is big and everybody is strong, so those things are a draw. Fundamentals are what determines who is successful on any given play. The saying is, "Low man wins." One way you master this concept as an offensive lineman is by practicing with chutes and boards.

Chutes are short, metal cages that offensive lineman bend over and crawl into. They get into their stance, and when the coach says so, they explode forward, simulating coming off the ball on a straight-ahead running play. The chute forces the player to stay low for a few steps, until he clears the structure and he can raise up his head without hitting the metal bars and getting a headache.

Did I mention that offensive lineman hate the chutes? Even back in high school, we despised them so much we snuck onto the practice field late one night, disassembled them, threw them in the back of a pickup truck and hid them in my backyard until the season was over.

Professional NFLers know better. They practice with chutes because they work. They might be uncomfortable, they might be hard, but they do work. They help you in mastering the fundamental of leverage. And this is something you need to constantly practice everyday because it's always important.

Less painful, but equally tedious, are the boards. In the good old days, the boards were just that, wooden boards, a foot wide and 10 feet long.

ROGER GOODELL

"Adversity has a way of introducing you to yourself. When you have to stand alone in making a decision, you discover the depth of your character."

Today, they are typically made of rubber, but the goal is the same: You spread your feet out so the board runs underneath you. With the board between your feet you practice executing your blocks, the board ensuring that you keep a good, wide, powerful, sturdy base at all times. With the board under you, it's impossible to bring your feet together, which is a major sin for an offensive lineman because you lose all your power and balance.

In concept, it seems easy

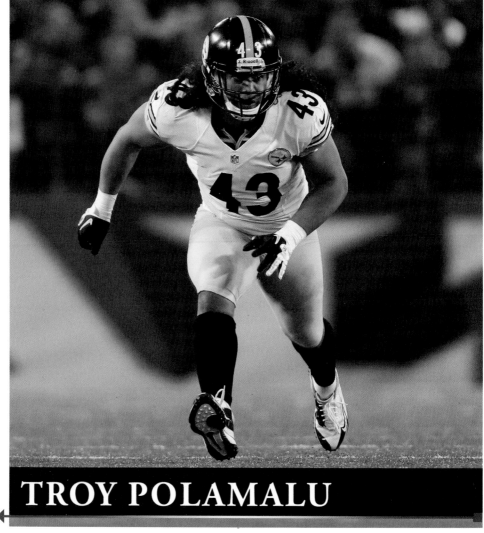

"Building character is just like working out. You build up and build up and you practice discipline and you get stronger. I build it up just like I condition my body as an athlete."

TROY POLAMALU

to get low and gain leverage, but it takes commitment and repetition. Chutes and boards are not high-tech or cutting-edge. They are very basic and have been around since football was invented. But that's because the fundamentals never change, only your attention to them does. The great thing about fundamentals is that they might not be sexy, but they work.

Great players understand that their skills and their game is a constant work in progress, from the day they start playing, until the day they retire. You never "got it" to the point where you neglect the fundamentals, or don't give them their due. Harbs used to remind us of a quote that really spoke to me as an older player: "It does not matter that I have done it 1,000 times before. What matters is that I am doing it again." It's a great reminder that up to this point, it doesn't really matter. What's important is that you keep working and keep striving to be your best.

"Building character is just like working out. You build up and build up and you practice discipline and you get stronger. I build it up just like I condition my body as an athlete." –TROY POLAMALU

If you're willing to invest the work required to master the fundamentals, you can achieve excellence. I never saw a great player who wasn't a master of the fundamentals. Sure, they would do amazing things all the time and end up on Sportscenter, but it all stemmed from the basics. Great football players make the routine plays routinely. That's true for the football field, and it's true for your character development for the rest of your life.

The Fundamentals of Character

When I think about the fundamentals of character that are most important to me, there are four that I work hard to master:

Great players understand that their skills and their game is a constant work in progress.

Wisdom: Being wise is not having all the answers. Actually, it's the contrary. When facing an important decision, a wise person does three things: seeks counsel, makes judgment, and takes action. This is not just to prevent you from looking like a fool; if others witness this modus operandi, they will be encouraged and confident in the decisions you make because of the wisdom you displayed.

Respect: Showing and giving respect to everybody the same is not only the right thing to do, but it's the sure-fire way to gain the respect of others. Albert Einstein said, "I talk to everybody the same, whether they are the president of the university or the custodian." That's a great rule to live by. Judge no one. A man or woman of character will be fair with everyone and seek justice for the "little people" who can't stand up for themselves.

Self-Control: Many things tempt us—money, status, sex, food, technology, pride, and selfishness to name a few.

A person of character has the inner strength to not be enslaved or controlled by these things. Too much of just about anything is a bad thing. People of character exemplify balance and a calmness about them. They will not be overtaken by impulse. Their actions are based on values, not whims.

Courage: Being courageous is doing what is right, all the time, no matter what. This is easy to say and may be hard to do, but if it were easy, it wouldn't be on the list, and it wouldn't be so uncommon. In today's culture of relativism, we are discouraged to stand up for what we believe in because we are told it might offend someone else. The truth might be inconvenient or unpleasant for some, but it's not mean or hurtful. It's simply the truth. And it's worth fighting for. I can't say I remember anyone regretting standing up for something that was really important to them, but I have regretted times in my own life where I did not speak up.

ANQUAN BOLDIN

"Character is at the center of what I strive for as a human being. I want to influence as many people as possible in a positive way. Character is at the core of that."

Why is it important to be wise, show respect, practice self-control, and act with courage? Because these things will develop your character, making you more consistent and stable. The more consistent and stable you are, the more people will trust you, and with trust, you become a person worth following. You want to be a leader, don't you? A leader of your family? Your community? Your company? Leaders are in high demand right now, and there also happens to be a huge shortage of them. Work on these fundamentals to develop your character.

> **"Character is at the center of what I strive for as a human being. I want to influence as many people as possible in a positive way. Character is at the core of that."**
> **–ANQUAN BOLDIN**

Greatness through Discipline

Literally millions of people know about Michael Oher from a 2006 book and a 2009 movie, both of them titled *The Blind Side.* About the only thing I knew about Michael when he showed up at the Ravens was that he was a first-round draft pick. As a veteran, I saw many first-rounders come and go, season after season, and many never lived up to the hype or promise. I didn't care about where he was drafted, and I didn't have time to watch his movie. He was going to have to prove it to me that he had what it took to make it in the NFL. It didn't take long.

I prided myself on being an early riser and the first one in the locker room in the morning. Our first team meeting in Baltimore was at 8 a.m., so I thought 6:30 a.m. was an appropriate time to get to work and start the day. When I arrived at that time the first day of practice, I was more than a little surprised and upset that there was a car already in the parking lot. I went into the locker room and there was

Mike, looking like he had been there for a while.

I assured myself that Mike would quickly fade once he got more comfortable, but I still decided to arrive the next day at 6:20 a.m. Again, Mike was already there.

The next day, I got to the locker room at 6:10 a.m. You know the story.

For the four years Michael and I were teammates, we had a friendly competition to see who would be the first to get to work. Our competition was based on a deep respect between two men who were totally committed to discipline and a demanding work ethic.

On the somewhat rare occasions when Mike would hit the snooze button an extra time and I did beat him into work, I would celebrate and let him know. "Hey, you're slippin', man!"

It would truly bother him, but it didn't change the fact that he was the hardest working guy on the team. Mike is proof that becoming a great football player takes work and commitment, but the effort is worth it.

You can often hear older people say that today's younger people don't have discipline or a work ethic. I suppose this is something older people have said forever. Still, I grow concerned when I see young men and women of great potential not succeeding because they lack discipline.

Discipline Is the Bridge

All of us have dreams, desires, and hopes about the kinds of lives we want to lead and the kinds of people we want to be. Men and women of character develop the discipline to turn dreams into realities.

Discipline is the bridge between goals and achievements.

Many people never learn this discipline because they need, or think they need, instant gratification. They want things that make them feel

The more consistent and stable you are, the more people will trust you, and with trust, you become a person worth following.

"Living with character is part of my duty in this life. Just get down to Earth and talk with people. Give yourself to them. That shows good character. It's almost like it becomes a habit. Having good character sets up a foundation for a lifetime."

ADRIAN PETERSON

good NOW! They don't have the time or patience for delayed gratification. They don't have the discipline to invest in goals that will take years of hard work to achieve.

I think discipline can be your secret weapon as you strive for excellence in all of life. The fact is, many people don't pursue excellence because it's just too damn hard. Well, guess what? If it's too hard for them, it's just right for you.

> **"Living with character is part of my duty in this life. Just get down to Earth and talk with people. Give yourself to them. That shows good character. It's almost like it becomes a habit. Having good character sets up a foundation for a lifetime."**
> **–ADRIAN PETERSON**

It's true that discipline isn't easy, like all the parties I skipped in college because hanging out late drinking beer was not going to be good for my workout the next morning. And discipline is hard, like

when I showed up at the house of Mike Morris for off-season workouts.

The coaches told me I needed to get stronger, and Mike was the guy to work out with. Mike was a long snapper for fourteen years in the NFL, but if there was an all-time NFL strength team, he would be the captain. He had a gorgeous gym in his basement, and he was gracious enough to invite me over to workout at the coaches' requests. Well, that first day, Mike really pushed me. I left Mike's house exhausted and embarrassed, but I was determined to get stronger, no matter what it took.

I woke up the next morning, hardly able to move and due at Mike's for another workout. My lower back was as tight as a drum. Well, I reminded myself of Friedrich Nietzsche's statement about things that don't kill us making us stronger. I decided the best thing to do was to go to Mike's and push through it.

I will always choose the pain of discipline over the pain of regret. Notice that it is, indeed, a choice.

What's in the Cup?

The choices you make now will show up in your behavior when the heat gets turned up. Try this exercise: Hold a cup full of water in your hand, and then shake the cup. What comes out? Water. Why? Because you are shaking it, right? Wrong. It's because there is water in the cup! What is inside of you will come out of you when you get shook up. Every time.

Most of the decisions most of us make affect only a few people, perhaps ourselves and our closest friends and family. But the decisions leaders make impact everyone they lead. I saw this clearly the day Coach Harbaugh came under fire in a team meeting.

It was October 2012, and we had just been hammered by the Houston Texans, losing 43-13 in an embarrassing game heading into our bye week. The game was supposed to be a contest between two of the best teams in the AFC, a preview of the championship perhaps. It turned into a beating. If it would have been a heavyweight boxing match, they would have stopped it.

The bye week is typically a time of the year to get a little breather, try to heal up as much as you can, and spend the latter part of the week at home and see what it's like to live a normal weekend. Before the team meeting where Harbs was going to lay out our practice plan for the week, someone caught wind that he was going to have us practice in pads during the bye. This was a little out of the ordinary, and was not welcome news in the locker room.

We went into the team meeting and Harbs told us what the workweek was going to consist of. "OK," he said, "I want us to go out and practice hard the next two days in pads."

"Why the hell are we doing that?" said one player, not trying to hide his disgust.

Then another jumped in, "Man, we are sore. We are beat up. We need rest, not practice in pads."

"That's a stupid idea," a third player piled on.

At this point, it was very uncomfortable in that meeting room. Harbs is a great coach and his players respect him. But I heard no respect in these comments, only aggression, opposition, and anger.

How would Harbs respond to these pre-meditated attacks? As a man of character, he knew not to respond to his players' anger with anger of his own.

"OK," he said. "Let's talk about this. I think we should practice in pads because we need the work. Why do you think we shouldn't?"

Guys gave plenty of reasons. Some valid, some not. Harbs sifted through the emotionally charged speeches of the players and concluded,

"OK. It obviously is important to you that we don't wear pads, so no pads." And then with a slight grin on his face he said, "But just for the record, I disagree."

"You've got to be wise in the way you deal with people. You can do it from an honest heart. Be upfront about who you are and what you stand for and what you're all about. Sometimes they say, 'Really?' And after a while, if you're consistent and true, they understand that what you say is important, and that your actions are the foundation underneath what you say. The result is that you become a person that people can trust."
–JOHN HARBAUGH

We've all been involved in similar situations when someone gets attacked and they go on the offensive. Pretty soon, the whole thing escalates and it gets really ugly. But Harbs stayed true to one of his leadership principles: *Attack problems, not people.* And he kept his focus when others attacked him. On this day, like so many others, Harbs responded from deep inside, not from the issues and emotions of the moment. Like the water and the cup, what was inside of Coach Harbaugh is what came out during the shake-up. That's what character can do for a leader.

Stuff Happens. Character Matters.

What about you? What does character mean to you? What fundamentals will you practice until they become your life habits? What kind of person do you want to be, and how can you be that person consistently through the good times and the bad times of life?

Difficult times test a person's character, as I experienced after that heartbreaking loss to the Patriots in the 2011 AFC Championship. But success tests character, too, as we can see when some pro players get lost in the money and celebrity that playing in the NFL can bring. Prosperity derails as many people as adversity. We don't always recognize success as a potential enemy.

No matter who you are, stuff is going to happen in your life. It could be good stuff, like winning the Super Bowl. Or it could be bad stuff, like losing the AFC Championship. Perhaps Helen Keller says it best. Her life story and her legacy bring power to words. "Character cannot be developed in ease and quiet. Only through experiences of trial and suffering can the soul be strengthened, vision cleared, ambition inspired, and success achieved."

The stuff of life will both test your character and reveal your character. You may not always like what you see when you look in the mirror, but you don't need to give up or give in.

"My dad was a horse trainer and my grandfather was a Marine Corps captain. They taught me to embrace hardship. Embrace adversity. Push through. At the end of the day, my character is the rock that I have to stand on. If you say you are going to do something, do it. No matter what."
–JARED ALLEN

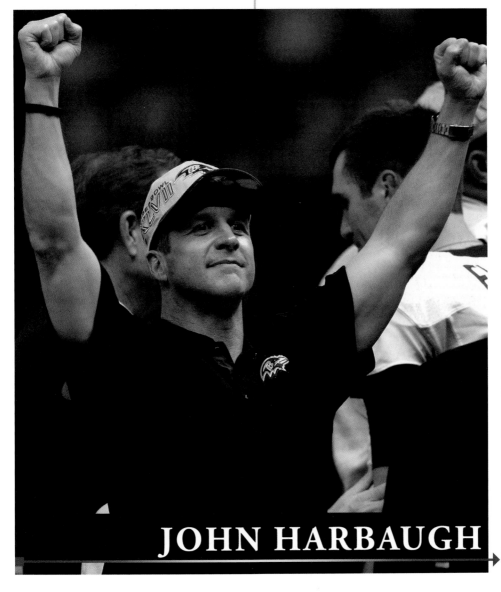

JOHN HARBAUGH

"You've got to be wise in the way you deal with people. Be upfront about who you are and what you stand for and what you're all about. The result is that you become a person that people can trust."

Life's moments of victory and defeat give you new chances to think about the kind of life you want to live. Your parents, teachers and coaches can't choose your character for you. Only you can choose what kind of person you want to be. And only you can choose to master the fundamentals that are required.

Stability and strength come through the development of character. When we develop our character, we become trustworthy, dependable, and consistent in our leadership, in our relationships, and in our life.

WHAT'S THE PAYOFF?

Choosing to deepen my CHARACTER gives me STABILITY to live with consistency.

CHAPTER FOUR

WHERE ARE YOU GOING?

"IF YOU DON'T KNOW WHERE YOU ARE GOING,
ANY PATH WILL GET YOU THERE."

–LEWIS CARROLL

CHOOSE TO CLARIFY YOUR GOALS

There are nearly 1,700 active players in the NFL, and just about every one of them dreams of winning the Super Bowl. But few of these dreams are fulfilled. In fact, every year, more than 1,600 NFL players fail to realize their Super Bowl dreams.

I know it was my goal to win the Super Bowl, but that didn't happen for fourteen seasons. Some would say that means I was a failure.

Why do some players and teams win, while others lose? It's not necessarily about dreaming harder or wanting it more. It's about setting clearly defined and realistic goals that are attached to detailed plans and action steps that you must take to reach those goals.

The way this worked for me during my seasons in the NFL involved translating my big dreams into hundreds of small action steps. My personal goal was to be the best player possible, to reach my full 100 percent potential. I translated that into action steps that I could work on every day.

Do you have a focus that allows you to direct your talents, or do you tend to continually change your goals and intentions?

Big Goals. Small Steps. Every Day.

One step toward my goals was getting eight hours of sleep a night. That sounds pretty elementary but sleeping is one of the best things you can do for your body. Still, many people neglect this and wind up sleep-deprived, and thus they are unable to perform at their highest level. I didn't want that to happen to me, so I wrote down my goal in my notebook: "Eight hours of sleep." Then I checked myself every day to make sure I was successful in this one small step. If I failed to get the desired night's sleep one night, I did what I could to make sure I got the full eight hours the next day.

A second small step I took was regulating my diet. I knew I wanted to eat 300 grams of protein a day to keep up my size and strength. So I wrote "300 grams of protein" in my notebook and checked myself every day to make sure I was eating enough of the right things.

Another step I took was to focus on a particular aspect of my performance during practices. There were many days when I would say, "OK, today in practice I'm going to make sure I take a great first step on every play," or "I'm going to be perfect on my combination blocks," or "I'm going to take great pass sets." This was very helpful, because it helped me focus on specific areas of my workout that needed attention, and it kept me from worrying about all the other aspects of my play. If you worry about everything generally, you accomplish nothing specifically.

Some of these goals might seem minute or ridiculous, but I didn't want to leave anything to chance. You only get one shot in the NFL. I felt like these small things were actually the big things. It's ridiculous to think I could have gotten my body to perform at its absolute peak without adequate rest and proper nutrition. As one of my former coaches, Brad Childress, used to say, "It gives you a chance to have a chance."

Some of my goals were more difficult to achieve. I wanted to bench press 500 pounds and squat 700 pounds. These goals required me to spend even more time in the weight room, fine tuning my technique and increasing my strength.

I translated my big dreams into hundreds of small action steps.

You can ask any of the people I played with. There was nobody more short-term goal oriented than me! I made detailed lists about what and when I would eat, how many days I would work out, how much time I would spend in the weight room, how many laps I would run around the field, and how many minutes I would stretch.

At the end of every day, I would check my lists in my notebook and compare them to my performance so I could see what I had accomplished and what I had failed to do. Then I would make new lists for the next day to make sure I was taking the small steps I needed to take to become the biggest, strongest, best football player I could be.

I didn't sit around dreaming about what it would feel like to have a Super Bowl ring on my finger. I spelled out the steps I needed to accomplish to achieve that goal, and worked on them every day.

Anybody in the world can use these simple techniques I used to pursue their goals step-by-step, day-by-day.

> **"My grandfather did not just believe in me and just inspire me to dream big, he actually chased those dreams with me. He gave me the inner belief that I was created to be successful. To not only do it the right way, but do it the right way in every circumstance, every time, every day of my life." –JASON WITTEN**

I know that some of this may sound terribly boring and routine, but that's the point! It's great to dream of winning the Super Bowl, but that game happens only once a year. What are you supposed to do the other 364 days of the year? Work on focusing your efforts in a very specific way.

> **"Focus is the glue that holds a goal in place. If you've got a great goal but not focus, you really**

don't have much."
—**GARY RYAN BLAIR**

I found that spelling out my goals in my mind and writing them down in my notebook helped me work toward these goals every day by taking the smaller steps that prepared me for the big game.

Dreamers or Doers?

When pollsters from the Pew Research Center asked young people between the ages of eighteen and twenty-five about their dreams for the future, 81 percent said they wanted to be rich and famous.

Other life goals fared less well. Only 30 percent of members of Generation Y said "helping others" was an important life goal. There were even fewer who wanted to be community leaders (22 percent) or become more spiritual (10 percent).

How many of these young people are going to reach their goals of wealth and fame? I bet it will be less than 81 percent! That's because there's a huge difference between dreaming and doing. Many people may dream of being rich and famous, but how are they actually going to make those dreams come true?

"How?" questions are very important. After all, it is easy to dream big, but what's the game plan for making these dreams real? Here's how I answer that question:

Discipline is the bridge between dreams and reality. Between goals and achievement.

Some people seem to achieve more of their goals than other people do. Is this because these people are special? Because they are different from everyone else? Because they were given an extra ounce of success juice at birth?

I have spent much of my life around successful people, so I can let you in on a secret. Their success was not given to them. They earned it through hard work.

*"My grand-
father did
not just
believe in
me and
just inspire
me to
dream big,
he actually
chased
those
dreams
with me.
He gave
me the
inner belief
that I was
created to
be suc-
cessful. To
not only do
it the right
way, but
do it the
right way in
every cir-
cumstance,
every time,
every day
of my life."*

JASON WITTEN

Here's something else I learned and wrote in my notebook:

Willpower is like a muscle. You can strengthen it over time.

Every off-season year I asked myself, "How am I going to improve from last year?" I didn't search high and low for the new fad training technique or nutritional supplement. I looked at my regimen and identified areas where I could become more disciplined. Can I train harder? Can I take better care of my body? I looked at everything I was already doing before I asked for anyone else's opinion. You have to be brutally honest with yourself if you want to get better. I have had many dreams for my own life. Some never happened. But some of my dreams have come true far beyond my wildest expectations.

Everyone has dreams, but do you want your dreams to come true? Then get to work on making them happen with discipline and willpower.

Goals Help You Focus

Most offensive linemen are okay with the fact that they are largely unknown to everyone except the most devoted football fans, but I found myself in the headlines in early 2012, and I was glad to be there.

The cause of my sudden (and brief) bout with fame was simple: I had just been named the Walter Payton NFL Man of the Year.

Every year, each of the thirty-two NFL teams nominates a player for this national award, which honors a player's work, both on and off the field. Now, here I was receiving an honor that was previously given to esteemed players like Junior Seau, Boomer Esiason, Troy Aikman, Dan Marino, Cris Carter, Jerome Bettis, Peyton Manning, Drew Brees, LaDainian Tomlinson, and Kurt Warner.

I didn't set out to win the Man of the Year Award.

My goal was to offer programs and encouragement to kids, helping them to achieve in school so they could be successful in life. There are hundreds of guys in the NFL who are deserving of the Walter Payton Award every year, but they just so happened to choose me.

Receiving this high honor from the NFL community was a highlight of my career, but I am not mentioning this award to pat myself on the back. I mention it to ask you an important question:

If you have chosen what kind of person you want to be, what steps are you taking to be that kind of person?

Winners focus on execution. Losers focus on results.

In other words, if my dream is playing in the NFL, I need to focus my energies on the things I can control (execution), not the things that are beyond my control (results).

Here's another way of saying it. Results are an outcome, and most of the time I cannot control how things turn out. Execution is about input, and almost always I can control what I will put into my goals every day. If I focus on controlling my input, the outcome will take care of itself.

The difference between focusing on results and execution may seem small and insignificant, but it's huge. I can't control who will win February's Super Bowl, but I can control what I do every day to prepare for that opportunity.

And even though my goal of winning the Super Bowl was very important to me, that was not my only goal in life. I wanted to be a better person. I wanted to have a positive impact in the world. It was these other goals that I believe led to my winning the Walter Payton NFL Man of the Year award.

When we take our talents and efforts and bring them together toward a goal, something powerful occurs. This is true in nature as well.

"The sun's rays do not burn until brought into focus." –ALEXANDER GRAHAM BELL

Half-Time Surprise

It was January 2013, and here we were again, facing off against the New England Patriots on their home turf in Foxborough, Massachusetts, for the AFC championship.

The Ravens had been here before, exactly one year earlier, and that AFC Championship game was a heartbreaking loss.

A loss like the one for the AFC Championship sticks with you for long, long time. So when we had one more chance to face them again in another championship game, we did what we always did— we focused on our preparation, not on New England.

We would depend equally on the legs of Ray Rice and the arm of Joe Flacco, balancing the running and passing games

in an effort to keep the Patriots' defense guessing.

But by halftime, Coach Harbaugh could see that our balanced approach was not working well enough. We were behind 13-7 and faced a second half against one of the NFL's most explosive offenses.

"OK," coach told us in the locker room during halftime. "Change of plans. In the second half we are going to let the ball fly."

Coach turned and looked at quarterback Joe Flacco. "We're going to turn you loose," he said. "I want you to throw on every down."

You might expect that the players would question such a dramatic change of plans. We were substituting a 50/50 balanced approach for an attack focused primarily on the pass. But that's what you do at halftime. You assess what's working and what isn't, and you make adjustments. You identify what changes, going forward, will give you the best chance to win the game. Your goal doesn't change, but the means of accomplishing it does. Things rarely go according to plan.

But there was no arguing or debating in the locker room that day. We trusted Coach Harbaugh, and even though it was very unusual for him to make such a radical change halfway through a game, we accepted our new marching orders and headed into the second half with a renewed sense of confidence and mission.

Thankfully, the new plan worked better than anyone would've ever imagined. Flacco threw three touchdown passes in the second half, completing the game with a stellar 106.2 passer rating. Meanwhile, our defense held the Patriots scoreless during the final thirty minutes, giving us a 28-13 victory that avenged our loss from the previous year, and paved our way to an appearance in the Super Bowl.

Joe Flacco is even-keeled, dependable, predictable, unflappable. By looking at him, you don't know if he has just thrown four touchdowns or four interceptions. Joe is the same every day, every practice, every game. That's why he is such a good leader. He's not up and down. We always consistently knew what Joe was going to bring, every day, every play. When Coach Harbaugh made the dramatic change in game plan at halftime, Joe took it in stride. He is truly comfortable in his own skin, and confident in his convictions.

"It's important that you know what you believe and stand firm in that. People aren't always going to agree with you or share your same views, but if they know what you are about they will respect you."
—JOE FLACCO

The hometown fans in Foxborough were shocked, while the Ravens' fans jumped for joy and hailed Coach

Harbaugh's change of plans as a brilliant strategic move. We all know that no one would have praised Harbaugh's brilliance if his revised game plan had led to defeat. He would have been crucified in the media and condemned by fans as a wild gambler who abandoned his game plan mid-course, only to suffer defeat once again.

The lesson we learned in Foxborough that day was simple. While it may be jarring and confusing to suddenly switch from Game Plan A to Game Plan B, pursuing a clearly defined goal may require a radical half-time change of plans, plus a lot of courage.

No professional team would ever start a game without a game plan, but once the game begins, things happen.

It never goes according to plan. Reality intrudes on your carefully made plans. Don't try to predict how it is going to go. Just prepare, and then go play. Even though your plans may change, your goal remains the same: Winning.

Each of us has goals in life. Some of us even have plans that help us pursue those goals. That's great, but when life lets you know that your plans aren't working out, don't give up on your goal. Instead, you need to come up with a revised plan for reaching that goal.

> **"I learned many powerful lessons from my dad, who was a U.S. Senator. One of those lessons is that in order to stay true to your goals, to be true to your convictions, you may have to pay a price. That is a powerful example of commitment and resolve. You have to be clear about your goals, and then stay focused, no matter what."**
> **–ROGER GOODELL**

What's Important Now

"Don't tell me, show me!"

These five simple words captured a lot of my dad's

philosophy of life, and he said them to me as often as I needed to hear them.

I remember one time when I was trying to persuade my dad that there were really good reasons why I had not cut the grass yet. Then I promised him that I would cut the grass just as soon as I could. Cross my heart.

"Don't tell me, show me!" he said.

With those five words he challenged me to quit flapping my jaws and start firing up the lawn mower.

Dreams are important. Our lives would be empty without them. But dreams don't change the world unless they are put into action. That's where goals come in. Goals help us convert lofty dreams into doable acts.

Some people dream of winning the lottery, even though the chances of doing so are one in millions. No matter how many tickets you buy, the odds are stacked against you.

Doers don't waste much time dreaming about buckets of gold found under rainbows or through a lottery ticket. They are too focused on taking the small, daily steps that will take them closer to their goals.

On the Ravens, we had a name for this focus on the small, daily details. We called it W.I.N., which stands for "What's Important Now?"

During the run-up to the championship game, Ravens players practiced W.I.N. by focusing on the things we could control. If it was a Wednesday, our goal was to have the best Wednesday practice in the history of our team. If we were scheduled to have a meeting to go over the playbook, we determined to have the best meeting ever. Pretty soon we were applying the W.I.N. approach to everything: having the best workout possible and eating the best breakfasts and lunches we could get our hands on.

Are you facing a significant challenge or obstacle in your life? Then focus on W.I.N.

JOE FLACCO

"It's important that you know what you believe and stand firm in that. People aren't always going to agree with you or share your same views, but if they know what you are about they will respect you."

"I learned many powerful lessons from my dad, who was a U.S. Senator. One of those lessons is that in order to stay true to your goals, to be true to your convictions, you may have to pay a price. That is a powerful example of commitment and resolve. You have to be clear about your goals, and then stay focused, no matter what."

ROGER GOODELL

"There is a man named Nathaniel in the Bible. Jesus said that Nathaniel was a man without guile. I have thought about what it means to be without guile. It means not to have deceit, not to have an agenda of trying to pull the wool over someone's eyes. You can trust a person that is without guile. That's a goal of mine."

JOHN HARBAUGH

Instead of allowing yourself to become overcome by the many demands and needs vying for your attention, bring some focus to your game by focusing on What's Important Now!

"There is a man named Nathaniel in the Bible. Jesus said that Nathaniel was a man without guile. I have thought about what it means to be without guile. It means not to have deceit, not to have an agenda of trying to pull the wool over someone's eyes. You can trust a person that is without guile. That's a goal of mine."
–COACH JOHN HARBAUGH

Life Changes. Goals Remain.

When I was eighteen, I thought I had everything figured out. At that point, my life plan was simple. Start a career. Get married. Buy a house with a white picket fence. Have 2.5 kids and a nice dog. And live happily ever after.

That was not the way things turned out for me, and I couldn't be happier about it. God apparently had something much better in store for me!

Now I see that life is much bigger and deeper than I understood at age eighteen. I still have goals that I am pursuing, but these goals continue to evolve as I live my life and face the tragedies, victories and other circumstances life brings my way.

Has anybody's life turned out the way they imagined it would?

Do you know anybody who has been able to create a game plan for life that never required tweaking?

Some people say: "Instead of making all these plans and changing them all of the time, why don't you just go with the flow?"

But giving in to the flow of life won't get you where you want to go. The only way to succeed in life is to develop the best goals you can and pursue them, step-by-step, with everything you've got today.

"I've tried to advance in the mold of Bart Starr. The first thing that you hear about him is not the way he played on the field, but that he is a man of high integrity, high character, high moral values and standards. That is the legacy that I aspire to leave. Deep down, I am content. I have what the world considers success, but that is not what fulfills me, and I think that people can relate to that."
–AARON RODGERS

Who knows what tomorrow may bring? That's not something we can control. The only thing we can control is what we do today. That's why I'm going to focus my energy on pursuing the goals I have set out for myself.

Needing to adjust in order to achieve a goal that I have set makes the ultimate accomplishment that is much more satisfying.

If I am able to develop a focus on goals every single day, my heart's dreams will have a much better chance of becoming reality.

The goals that we choose for our life and the path that leads us there will determine our ultimate destination. While the journey may be filled with complication and obstacles, a goal carefully chosen will help us to keep our focus, and bring assurance that the impact of our work and our life will land right where we intend.

WHAT'S THE PAYOFF?

Choosing to clarify my GOALS gives me FOCUS to direct my gifts and skills.

CHAPTER FIVE

WHERE CAN YOU FIND STRENGTH GREATER THAN YOURSELF?

"SELF AS SOURCE IS A VERY SMALL REALITY."

–FATHER JEFF HUARD

CHOOSE TO CONNECT WITH POWER

It's another Sunday afternoon, and millions of people around the country are settling into comfy recliners or sofas to watch NFL football on TV. For some games, more than 25 million people are tuning in.

Of course, stadiums around the league are packed, holding 60,000–100,000 football-loving people.

One of the fans' favorite moments is when they see their team emerging from the tunnel and running down the field. Their entrance is accompanied by various kinds of pre-game hoopla, which may include cheerleaders cheering, mascots mugging, fireworks exploding, flames shooting skyward, loudspeakers pumping out bass-heavy music, or even Air Force jets screaming high overhead.

Some players pump their fists as they run to the sidelines. Some raise their hands in salute to their fans. Some jump up and down to burn off excess energy. Meanwhile, the crowd goes wild.

But in the final moments before they hit the field, players are taking advantage of their last few seconds of silence so they can calm their minds, mentally review a few plays, think about how best to foil their opponents, and prepare themselves for the intense three hours that lie ahead.

Sure, locker rooms can be noisy places at most times, but during those precious final few minutes before game time, most players prefer things dead quiet. That's because we're wondering what challenges we will face on the field today.

We ask ourselves questions like these:

Will I play well?

Will we be victorious?

Will I survive the punishment that is waiting for me out on the field?

Will this be the day my ankles, knees, or neck will be bent and twisted in ways they aren't supposed to be bent and twisted, forcing me to be taken out of the game I love for a few minutes, a few months, or forever?

There was never any question that each and every game would be tough. The only question before game time was how tough *this* particular game would be.

I will admit: There was not a single game during my fifteen years in the NFL when I wasn't tense and uneasy right before we ran out onto the field.

And on those many Sunday mornings when I got out of bed and my foot hit the floor and I didn't feel particularly spry, I wondered, "How in the world am I going to play a game today? Will this be my last day playing in the NFL?"

During my seasons with the Ravens, the one thing that would ease my anxious mind and racing heart was just before we were about to take the field, Coach Harbaugh would call everybody to circle up in the locker room, we would all join hands, and one of the players would lead us in prayer.

Most times the prayers followed a similar format: They began by thanking the Almighty for giving all of us another day and the wonderful privilege of playing in the NFL. Then we prayed for the safety of all the players, on both teams. Then we would state that victory was not our number one objective, but rather that God would be glorified through our efforts on the field. The gist of the ending of the prayer was always the same.

"Let your will be done, Lord."

I can clearly remember the hundreds of times I prayed that last phrase silently to myself before running out into the crazy, chaotic environment of a fan-filled stadium.

Where do you turn when you are about to face a challenge that seems far beyond your abilities?

Where do you channel your emotions when you are white with fear?

That brief phrase, "Let your will be done, Lord" has been the prayer of my life for as long as I can remember. It's a simple prayer, but it helps me connect with a power that's much greater than myself. And when I do that, I have a supernatural strength that helps me overcome my own limitations.

"I have always been very disciplined, always calling on God's name knowing that whatever circumstance that I was facing in my life that I could always rely on God to give me strength."
–TROY POLAMALU

Do you have the strength to overcome the nagging weaknesses in your life, or do you find that you are constantly pushed back and diverted from your dreams?

The Bonds of Brothers

An important source of strength in our lives is the power that comes from being connected with other people. I repeatedly experienced this kind of power during my fifteen years in the NFL.

One of the quotations I wrote down in my notebooks was:

"One is too small a number for greatness."

I could not agree more. The men I played with in the NFL helped me achieve greatness, and I helped them, too. The bonds I developed with these brothers were another source of power in my life.

My teammates and I gave each other encouragement, strength, and a sense that we were pursuing a higher purpose together than we did on our own. These bonds between me and my NFL brothers gave me strength in three unique ways.

First of all, I loved them and did not want to let them down. I knew that when a pass was called in the huddle that there was no way I was going to let my guy put a hand on Joe Flacco. Or if it was a run play, I was determined to open a hole for Adrian Peterson, or die trying! My commitment to them and desire to be there for them gave me a sense of determination and energy that I would not have had on my own.

A second way my brothers gave me power was by their resilience. In the NFL, everybody gets beat up week after week. Sure, sometimes we complained and whined, but when it was time to go, it was

time to go. Guys in the NFL answer the bell, regardless of how they feel. Somehow, they put the physical pain aside and take the field on Sundays (or Mondays or Thursdays). The guys I had the honor of playing alongside were tough, mentally and physically, and they kept going, week after week, and by doing so they inspired me to keep going, too.

Third, my brothers empowered me to be my best by encouraging me to push myself as hard as I could and by showing me by example exactly how that was done.

From the first day I arrived in the NFL, I was surrounded by All-Pro players who had a never-ending desire to improve their game, and they relentlessly pushed themselves to achieve that goal. I never would have become an All-Pro player myself without these examples around me, encouraging me and pushing me to give my very best every day.

And it wasn't just star players who helped me as brothers.

It was all players, even those at the bottom of the roster that empowered me.

Each NFL team has fifty-three players on its roster. Every week, forty-six of those players suit up, and twenty-five are starters (eleven on offense, eleven on defense, and three on special teams).

There are always a handful of players on each team who get most of the attention from the fans and the media. That's understandable. People are going to talk more about the quarterback than the guy who snaps him the ball.

But we shouldn't let the NFL's star-studded celebrity system make us forget that all forty-six players are important and have something to contribute, even if it's player number forty-six down at the bottom of the team roster.

Here's a trivia question for you: Who made the final tackle in the 2013 Super Bowl? I'm going to save you some time and tell you: It was Josh Bynes, the linebacker who had anchored Auburn's dominant defense and had joined the Ravens as an undrafted free agent in 2010.

Josh has had to earn every minute of playing time in the NFL. He has been "cut" by the Ravens more than a couple times, going back and forth between the practice squad and active roster. In training camp in 2012, he fractured a vertebrae in his back during practice. I would see him in the locker room in an upper body cast or brace of some sort, laboring to move in any direction, and I figured his career was over. He had earned his "purple heart" (and I mean no disrespect to any servicemen or women. It is a term of respect in the NFL that refers to players whose careers ended because of serious injury). Well, I was dead wrong. Josh persevered, and on the last play of the Super Bowl, the Ravens free-kicked to the San Francisco 49ers. The 49ers' Ted Ginn, Jr., caught the ball and started running. It was Josh who tackled Ted, ending the game and sealing our victory.

It was not a particularly heroic or game-saving tackle, but when Josh was given an assignment to do, he executed it flawlessly. For me, his performance is a powerful symbol of the deep bonds forged between each and every player on the team, even those players who are less-well-known than the superstars. While the media wanted to focus on the Super Bowl being the end of Ray Lewis's illustrious career, or who was going to Disneyworld, they missed something that we could all take something from. Most of us probably can relate more to Josh and his situation than to Ray Lewis.

Just being a part of a team with guys like Josh gave me power to go beyond my personal limitations.

"Family is very import-ant to me. My wife, kids, parents, brothers, sister - all of them are strength for me. If one of them has a problem, it's my prob-lem as well. Some things come and go, but we will be family forever."
–JOE FLACCO

Your Connection with Power

What actually happens when people pray? Theologians have debated this question for centuries, so I'm not sure I can answer it precisely. But I do know two things:

First of all, I know that when I pray, I am not alone in facing my challenges and problems in life, and that God is somehow with me, helping me.

Second, I have seen that when people ask God for help, help seems to arrive. That help doesn't always come as soon as they want it to, and it doesn't always come in the specific ways they imagined it might. But help does eventually come, as I saw for myself while helping a family member caught up in drug addiction.

Sam (that's not his real

"Family is very important to me. My wife, kids, parents, brothers, sister- all of them are strength for me. If one of them has a problem, it's my problem as well. Some things come and go, but we will be family forever."

JOE FLACCO

name) had struggled with addiction for years. It's probably more accurate to say he had lost the struggle, for in the battle between Sam and drugs, the drugs were clearly winning.

Addiction is a powerful problem that affects many people, and there are many clinics promising to help addicts recover, as I discovered when trying to help Sam find a place that might work for him.

I helped Sam go to one two-week clinic, but he fought everything they tried to do, so nothing really worked. As soon as his two weeks were up, he returned to abusing drugs.

Later, I helped Sam find a month-long program. "I'm really serious this time," he told me. I wanted to believe him, but after everything we had been through, I found it difficult to trust him anymore. After the month was up, Sam again returned to his old ways.

If you have ever known someone dealing with drug or alcohol addiction, you know it can be a depressing and seemingly hopeless situation. But even when I had lost hope in Sam's ability to help himself, I never lost hope in God's ability to help Sam, if only Sam would seek His help.

That's what finally happened. After the latest in a years-long series of drug-induced outbursts and craziness, Sam eventually reached the end of his road.

"I don't know how it happened," he told me, "but I found myself naked and on my knees with nowhere else to turn. So I turned to God and asked him for help."

Sam joined a recovery program based on a similar approach to the twelve steps developed by Alcoholics Anonymous. AA is based on the belief that overcoming addiction requires the help of a Higher Power (aka God). We had spent thousands of dollars on programs based on science, and with no success. This program was based on the need for God, and now Sam is rock solid.

After years of trying everything under the sun, Sam found the power of God, and he has been drug-free for a couple of years. Sam isn't necessarily a religious person, but he is spiritual, and he realizes he needed oversized help to escape the clutches of his addiction.

So is everything now totally A-OK for Sam? Far from it. Today he sits in a federal prison, serving time for a crime he committed while strung out on drugs.

Does that mean prayer doesn't work? I don't think so. I believe God *has* answered many of Sam's prayers, as well as the many prayers of mine, and those of the many other family members who prayed for him for so long. I believe these prayers made a huge difference in his life, even if it was impossible to untangle all the old messes Sam had gotten himself into during the years he was an addict.

Only God truly knows what happens in these scenarios. Meanwhile, I have experienced "a source of strength greater than myself" in my own life, and have seen it in Sam's life as well.

> **"I will never push my faith on anybody. If you have a problem, I'm not going to tell you how to beat it, how to beat the clock. If you want to know, ask me, and I will try to lead you to the right source. I know where I go to find my answers. It is in God through Jesus Christ."**
> **–JARED ALLEN**

"How in the World Do You Do It?"

It was a Tuesday afternoon practice in November during my thirteenth NFL season, and I was standing on the sidelines trying to catch my breath. Around me were Anquan Boldin and Todd Heap, two Ravens teammates I greatly respected.

We were joined by Ben Grubbs, a fifth-year player who, like us, was feeling beaten up and worn down during a season that seemingly had no end.

Ben was having one of those days. I could see he was down, so I asked him, "Whats going on?" It was my invitation to let him know I was a little concerned.

He took a deep breath and he asked me, sincerely, "Birk, how have you been able to play so long in this league?"

It wasn't the first time I was faced with this question, but I rarely gave a thoughtful response because normally it was from a non-player, and with all due respect, they wouldn't understand because they don't know what an NFL player goes through on a daily basis. But this was Ben. He was my friend, my teammate, my brother. He played left guard, right next to me on the offensive line.

I thought for a moment because I wanted to answer the question correctly. I knew Ben was looking for some guidance, inspiration, and reassurance that everything was going to be alright.

"By the grace of God," was what came out of my mouth, and I was dead serious. I remember being a young player, when I wasn't thinking how many years I was going to play in the NFL. I wondered each day how I was going to make it through another twenty-four hours. The NFL is like the Navy Seals in the respect that "the only easy day was yesterday," and that's especially true for younger players. It was like I was fighting for my life every day. I would look at the vets in awe, thinking the same thing Ben was asking me. And as I look back on it, I really can't tell you how I did it. I mean, I would love to tell you that it's because I outworked everybody and took great care of myself (and that's true), but it doesn't explain how or why I lasted. All the work I put into being a football player only gave me a chance to have a chance. I definitely was not strong or tough enough to do it on my own. The reason I was able to endure all of it was because my strength came from somewhere other than me.

"The Bible is my favorite book. That's the one you need to make your favorite and have it with you at all times and go to it no matter what situation you are dealing with. You will find the answer there."
–ADRIAN PETERSON

Life Is Fragile

Not every player does survive. I remember being at the Vikings pre-season training camp in Mankato, Minnesota, on July 31, 2001, the day one of my most beloved teammates, Korey Stringer, fell to the ground.

We prayed for Korey, but he died the next morning from complications of heat stroke. We had a team meeting, but none of us knew what to say or do. One of our brothers was dead. We were mourning. Hard. We attended his funeral a few days later, hugged his widow, Kelcie, and told her we were sorry. And then we looked at his young son, Kodie, and I didn't know what to think. I had so many questions, so much sadness in my heart. The last thing any of us wanted to do was go back to playing football, but the season was going to happen. We had no idea how we were going to do it, but we had to go back to work. It was through prayer and dependence on God that we, as a team, were able to move on.

"I have found that the further I become removed from my heat source, my power source, which is God, the more empty I feel, and the more I allow falsehoods to enter into my life. But when I continue to stay close to God and keep my thoughts focused, I become more fine-tuned."
–TROY POLAMALU

But for me, some of the times when I have been most dependent on God's grace weren't even related to football. They were closer to home.

JARED ALLEN

"I will never push my faith on anybody. If you have a problem, I'm not going to tell you how to beat it, how to beat the clock. If you want to know, ask me, and I will try to lead you to the right source. I know where I go to find my answers. It is in God through Jesus Christ."

"The Bible is my favorite book. That's the one you need to make your favorite and have it with you at all times and go to it no matter what situation you are dealing with. You will find the answer there."

ADRIAN PETERSON

It was the afternoon of July 23, 2008, and I was celebrating my birthday with my daughters by sharing one last swim in the pool before heading off to training camp.

When a friend stopped by to wish me happy birthday, I chased the girls out of the pool. But a moment later, as I talked to my friend, I turned around to see a horrifying sight. My two-year-old daughter, Ava, had gotten back in the pool and she was motionless under the water.

I dove into the pool and pulled out her tiny body. She was barely conscious. I called 911, and when the ambulance arrived, I crawled in the back with my daughter and held her limp hand. By this time she had lost consciousness. It was only a ten-minute ride to the hospital, but time seemed to stretch and slow down.

The paramedics were working feverishly, taking her vitals and trying to revive her. Nothing was working, there were no positive signs.

I don't remember another time in my life when I ever felt so small and helpless. The only thing I could say was, "God help us. God help us."

When the ambulance finally pulled up to the emergency room exit, the paramedics jumped into action. And when they reached for the gurney that held my daughter and pulled it out of the ambulance door, a strange thing happened. As the legs of the gurney snapped into place and the big black wheels hit the pavement, my daughter suddenly woke up and started wailing.

That was the best thing I had seen since this nightmare started, but it wasn't the end. There were hours of tests to do, hours during which I continued to pray, "God help us."

Finally, a doctor came toward me as I sat in the waiting room.

"She's fine," she told me. "Everything is checking out. We want to keep her overnight for observation, but we're not worried at this point."

"What happened?" I asked.

"You know, I have no idea," the doctor told me. "I really can't explain it."

Life is fragile, and everything can change in a second. Whenever it seems like things are spiraling out of control or heading for certain disaster, I do what I can to help out, but I also realize I can't do everything. Sometimes it seems I can't do *anything*. That's why I regularly ask for God's help.

It is during some of life's darkest moments when I am utterly powerless that I am most aware that there is a power much greater than myself that sustains me and energizes me. I didn't need any proof that God was at work in my life, but when people ask me how I know God exists, I cite this incident. Who wouldn't want to be connected to such a power?

From "Help Me!" to "Thank You!"

It's another Sunday afternoon. The last seconds have ticked down on the play clock. The officials have blown their last whistle. Another NFL game has ended and entered the history books.

More fireworks explode. Fans of the winning team clap and scream and dance jigs, while fans of the losing team silently stream out of the stadium. I give big bear hugs and say, "Howyadoin'?" to guys from the other team who, ten minutes ago, were trying to decapitate me.

But as TV commentators commentate, a group of players and coaches are gathering at midfield.

Some days there are a dozen of us. Some days there are only a few. It doesn't matter.

We get together in a circle near the 50-yard line, get down on our aching knees, bow our sweaty heads, and hold each others' bandaged hands as someone leads us in a brief prayer that goes something like this:

"Thank you, God, for seeing us through another game. Thank you for the opportunity to serve

> ...
> **during life's darkest moments ... I am most aware of a power greater than myself ...**

"I have found that the further I become removed from my heat source, my power source, which is God, the more empty I feel, and the more I allow falsehoods to enter into my life. But when I continue to stay close to God and keep my thoughts focused, I become more fine-tuned."

TROY POLAMALU

"Life is fragile, and everything can change in a second. Whenever it seems like things are spiraling out of control, I do what I can, but I realize that I cannot do everything. Sometimes I can't do anything at all. That's why I regularly ask for God's help."

MATT BIRK

you with our talents. And be with our teammates who were injured today. We humbly ask for your continued blessings on us and our families. And may all of the glory go to you. Amen."

None of the players who lead these spontaneous post-game prayers talk about who won or who lost. It's not about that. In victory or in defeat, it's about stopping for a minute, tuning out the chaos around us, and connecting to the power source that gives us life. It's also about men who live in the spotlight turning that spotlight around and shining it on God, the true source of their power and glory.

Sometimes during these prayers I would open my eyes, look around at the bruised and aching guys who encircled me, and think:

"Wow. Look at these great men. I am so blessed to be able to play with and against them. What an honor."

These guys are some of the main reasons I am so grateful I played NFL football, and these brief times of post-game prayer provided some of the most amazing moments of every Sunday.

Who knows what tomorrow will bring? But I know that regardless of whether I am celebrating a Super Bowl victory or praying for my unconscious daughter in the back of a speeding ambulance, I want to remain connected to the source that gives me life and strength and power to live and love for another day.

When our life connects with a source of strength greater than ourselves, a power transfer occurs. Each of us is created to live our life's adventure with the strength, comfort, encouragement, resources, and power provided by God and others.

WHAT'S THE PAYOFF?

Choosing to connect with POWER greater than myself gives me the STRENGTH to overcome self-limitations.

CHAPTER SIX

WHO CAN GIVE YOU GUIDANCE?

"THE PESSIMIST COMPLAINS ABOUT THE WIND. THE OPTIMIST
EXPECTS IT TO CHANGE. THE REALIST ADJUSTS THE SAILS."
–WILLIAMS ARTHUR WARD

CHOOSE TO SEEK WISE COUNSEL

Excitement and fear. Those were the two emotions I felt as I started my rookie season in the NFL.

I was excited because playing in the NFL was a dream come true, and in my case, it was a dream that had always seemed highly unlikely. After all, how many Harvard players make it to the NFL?

That's why I had lined up a job as a Wall Street analyst that I would start after graduation. I wasn't certain whether my future was in finance or football. But the Minnesota Vikings made their opinion known when they drafted me in the sixth round of the 1998 draft.

That's when the fear kicked in.

When I compared myself to the NFL players whose ranks I was now joining, I worried that I didn't have the skill, the size, the strength, or the experience needed to match up against these proven professionals.

Sure, I had made it into the NFL, but now what? Would I survive my first season? Or would I be another in a long line of rookies who appear briefly, perhaps shine brightly for a few plays, but ultimately fail to make any impact, and are never heard from again?

That's why I am so grateful to the six men who became my guides, teachers, friends and mentors during my rookie season. For a young, anxious player like me, these men were an answer to my prayers.

I watched everything they did. I listened to everything they told me. I did everything they suggested I do in practice or in the weight room. And thanks to their wise counsel, I became the best player I could be.

Do you have guidance to help keep you on the right path, or are you trying to "go it alone"?

ROOKIE YEAR:

My Six Mentors

Let me introduce you to the six men who helped turn this fearful rookie into a NFL veteran.

· RANDALL MCDANIEL ·

Randall McDaniel was the true star of our offensive line, but he was a quiet star who didn't showboat or toot his own horn. Praised by many as one of the greatest offensive linemen in NFL history, Randall was a consistent player who started 202 consecutive games on his way to playing in twelve consecutive Pro Bowls. He was inducted into the Pro Football Hall of Fame in 2009.

Randall showed me what it meant to continually work to be better. Never one to rest on his laurels, he methodically went about his business, working hard every minute. Randall's deep commitment to excellence inspired me from day one.

· JEFF CHRISTY ·

All-Pro center Jeff Christy showed me you didn't have to have incredible size and strength to be an NFL center. Like me, Jeff was a smaller player, which made him play with a chip on his shoulder. There was not a tougher competitor. He demonstrated that if an undersized player like me could play smart and be tough, he could succeed in the NFL.

During my first two years on the team, I sat next to Jeff in meetings and he helped me understand everything in the playbook. We were also roommates on the road. He was very open with me, very patient

Thanks to their wise counsel, I became the best player I could be.

with me, and answered all my questions, no matter how silly they were.

· **KOREY STRINGER** ·

Tackle Korey Stringer showed me how to combine hard work

"Throughout my career, I never stopped seeking wise counsel from great players. Today, I still seek guidance from wise counselors, not about football, but about life. And I believe you need to do the same if you want to pursue greatness in your life."

MATT BIRK

and fun. He had a great sense of humor, but when it was time to get to work, nobody was more serious, more focused, or more intense, both during games and practice. (Sadly, Korey suffered from severe heat stroke during our 2001 training camp and died soon after.)

· TODD STEUSSIE ·

Pro Bowl left tackle Todd Steussie was a fellow weight room meathead. Both of us loved lifting heavy weights, doing ridiculous workouts, and getting as big and strong as we could. Todd showed me how to be a master of technique on the field, which he honed by repetition, repetition and more repetition of the fundamentals.

· DAVE DIXON ·

Dave Dixon was one of two NFL players who was a Maori (which is a Polynesian people group in New Zealand). A rugby player who later learned to play football, Dave inspired me by rising from the most humble beginnings, working

to turn his raw talent into true professionalism.

· MIKE TICE ·

Finally, offensive line coach Mike Tice knew the game inside and out, and he taught me mental and physical toughness. An option quarterback in college, Mike played fourteen seasons in the NFL as a tight end, although he was really like a sixth offensive lineman because he was on the field to block, not catch passes. He was one of those players who had to fight for his spot on the team every single year in training camp, then battle all season just to stay on the roster. As a coach, he had credibility because he had come up the hard way in the NFL as a player. I knew he would coach me hard and coach me right.

These six men showed me how to survive and thrive in the NFL, and I am convinced that it was their guidance and care that helped me survive early on in my career, and then ultimately "make it."

The lessons I learned from these guys I carried with me through my entire career. You could describe every one of these guys as a true professional.

Throughout my career, I never stopped seeking wise counsel from great players. Today, I still seek guidance from wise counselors, not about football, but about life. And I believe you need to do the same if you want to pursue greatness in your life.

Are You Strong Enough to Ask for Help?

You have probably heard stories about men who refuse to stop and ask for directions, even when they are hopelessly lost. Some men are too proud to ask anyone else for help. Others think asking for help is a sign of weakness or stupidity.

Not me. I believe it takes strength and courage to admit that I don't have all the answers and to ask someone else who knows more than I do.

That doesn't mean it's easy to seek guidance. Our culture emphasizes rugged individualism, the idea that each one of us should go it alone and chart our own individual course. This idea is symbolized by the lone cowboy riding his horse across the wide-open plains.

Life in the NFL often promotes individualism. Even though football is a team sport, a handful of big stars get much of the attention and credit. Big games are promoted as grudge matches between superstar quarterbacks like Joe Flacco and Tom Brady, not a competition between dozens of players on each team.

But the reality of life in the NFL doesn't resemble the advertising images. In fact, the best NFL players are the ones who are always seeking guidance from coaches, from fellow players, and from other wise counselors they can rely on.

I was privileged to play alongside Adrian Peterson for two years while I was still with the Vikings. Some people say that Adrian is the strongest player, pound for pound,

ADRIAN PETERSON

"When I am dealing with difficulties, I go to men of God from whom I get positive knowledge and great wisdom. When I am struggling with the situation and could use someone to talk to, it's those guys that I'm calling. I need to tear my pride down to the ground and not be ashamed to talk to someone about my problems."

of any player in the NFL. I wouldn't argue that. But he is not too strong or too proud to ask for guidance.

> "When I am dealing with difficulties, I go to men of God from whom I get positive knowledge and great wisdom. When I am struggling with the situation and could use someone to talk to, it's those guys that I'm calling. I need to tear my pride down to the ground and not be ashamed to talk to someone about my problems."
> **—ADRIAN PETERSON**

WANTED:

Mentors

I have found that many of the best players regularly reach out to others for guidance and counsel. Here's what Jared Allen has to say about seeking counsel:

> "I am willing to say, 'Hey I can't do this alone.' I need to find people with the same moral fiber to help me. They give me an outsider's perspective on how I can better myself and direct my energy. We all need to seek help in that way. My dad taught me that it is important to remove myself from the circumstance and speak to someone else and get a different perspective. Somebody that is neutral."
> **—JARED ALLEN**

Where can you find a mentor? I suppose you can do what a lot of people do and hire a life coach. But I have been able to surround myself with mentors who care for me and don't ask me to pay them for their guidance.

You have people in your life now who would be willing to offer you counsel if you ask them. Here are four characteristics that my four mentors seem to share:

1. **They're Wiser**

   One characteristic all my mentors

share is they are wiser than me. Age brings experience, and when I am seeking guidance for the challenges and issues and decisions I face in my life, I want input from somebody who has seen more and knows more than me.

All of my mentors have been tested by fire in their professional careers, their marriages, and their relationships with their kids. Along the way, they have gained valuable wisdom that they're more than willing to share with me. These wise men help keep my feet on the path.

2. They "Get It"

During my rookie season, the men who guided me were proven professionals who knew how to dominate the line of scrimmage. That was exactly what I needed then. Today, my mentors are experienced older men who've "got it." They have their lives in order. They are at a stage in life where they can show me how to pursue my dreams, and how to avoid dead ends.

This doesn't mean everything always goes perfectly for them, but they have been able to navigate the challenges and crises of life and wind up still standing strong. I admire them for what they have achieved. I respect how they live their lives. I want my own life to resemble theirs in ways both big and small.

3. The Faith Factor

The men I look up to and call on to guide me are godly men of faith. They don't merely talk about God, but demonstrate their commitment, priorities and values through their actions. These aren't guys who started going to church yesterday and now claim they have the God thing all figured out. These are men who have consistently walked the path for years and can show me what true faithfulness is all about.

4. Out of My League

Perhaps the most interesting characteristic of my mentors is that none of them were professional athletes. This did not happen by accident.

Don't get me wrong. I have sought guidance from fellow players for years and years. But there is more to life than sports, and having mentors with different kinds of life and career experience gives me a broader perspective than I could get from talking only with fellow athletes.

You are different from me and face different challenges in your life, so you might seek out different kinds of counsel than

I have. Still, you can't go wrong by surrounding yourself with wise, trustworthy, principled and experienced older mentors who can help you see what life is all about, and help you figure out how to live the best life you can.

An Anchor in Life's Chaos

I have lived a charmed life. It started with two loving parents who provided me with everything I needed (but not everything I wanted, thankfully). That's why I have such a deep respect for players like Jason Witten and Troy Polamalu. They did not have many of the good breaks that I had, but they displayed tremendous character by working hard to develop greatness as players and, more importantly, as men.

During our interviews, both Jason and Troy talked about the people in their life that gave them guidance and wise counsel, and set them on the right path. Their words tell the story:

> "When I was only twelve years old, I was moved to live in my grandfather's home. It was the first time in my life that I saw a lot of good things. He provided me with hope. He actually helped me to understand the quote: 'People don't care how much you know until they know how much you care.' Adversity happens in each of our lives. You got to have a tight circle of people that you can open up to and be honest with. Friends who are willing to say things that sometimes you don't want to hear. I remind myself that I need to train myself every day, today, to take criticism, take the correction. Not to get bitter, but to get better. That helps me to keep moving in the right direction."
> —JASON WITTEN

"Because of my life experience of being without parents, dealing with adoption, dealing with racism, gang violence and dealing with many challenging circumstances, I am able to speak with authenticity. It has always been my belief, and it has been in my heart, that in truth I have had the best guide of all, God. I thank God that my grandmother instilled into me a life of prayer."
–Troy Polamau

Who Knows You Best?

Two other sources have proven very reliable in my life. Sometimes other people know us better than we know ourselves. Who is the one person who knows me better than anyone else? That would be my wife, Adrianna.

All of us have our blind spots. That means we don't always see everything clearly. Sometimes our vision is clouded by our ego, fears, and emotions.

What we need is someone who knows us on a deep level and can see through our confusion. Someone who know us for who we really are and can speak love and truth into our lives. Someone who will tell us what we need to hear, not what we want to hear.

My wife is that person in my life. I'm glad I married someone who knows who she is and can remind me who I am when the world is going crazy.

But the one who truly knows me the very best is my Creator, the one who made me. He knows how I'm wired and what I'm supposed to do. He knows me better than I know myself. He is more than willing to guide me. All I have to do is seek His counsel.

"For me, God means everything. God keeps me grounded and helps me to understand that no matter what is going on, my destiny is always clear. I don't have to worry.

All of us have our blind spots.

**I don't have to fret. I know what my home is going to look like."
–ANQUAN BOLDIN**

Not all NFL players talk openly about faith, but faith is central for many of the All-Pro players I came to know during my career, and for those you are reading about in this book. In the NFL, a lot of guys are pursuing their faith. Faith is an anchor, and you really need that when you're in the chaos of the spotlight. I think that's one reason why so many players pray together before and after games. That's why so many attend worship services or Mass with team chaplains before games, or attend Bible studies during the week.

I remember seeking God's guidance with unusual intensity when I was out for the entire 2005 season due to injuries and surgeries (four in thirteen months).

I had started every game for more than four years, gone to Pro Bowls, signed the long-term contract—everything was going great. I was sailing along, and then I got injured.

I didn't know if I would ever play again. These were anxious times and I was a wreck. Things were not going according to plan. I was worried about what the future held.

Of course, God likes us to seek his guidance even when we're not in crisis. That's really what prayer is all about: reaching out to God so we may be able to hear His wise counsel. All he asks is for us to turn our lives over to Him. If we can do that on a daily basis, then we have nothing to worry about.

"We need to seek counsel. I try to seek counsel from as many people as I can, to include people and build perspective. If you quiet yourself and listen, whether it's an e-mail or something you read in the Bible or in the newspaper and you write it down as quick as you can. You pray for discernment and judgment and then, all of

"I try to seek counsel from as many people as I can .... If you quiet yourself and listen, ... and you write it down as quick as you can. You pray for discernment and judgment and then, all of a sudden, you say, 'Oh my gosh. That is perfect.'"

JOHN HARBAUGH

a sudden, you say, 'Oh my gosh. That is perfect.'"
—JOHN HARBAUGH

We're All Rookies!

I sought guidance during my rookie year and throughout my career in the NFL, and I continue to seek wise counsel from caring mentors today.

AARON RODGERS

"I try to seek out advice along the way from people who have more life experience than myself. I find it vital to lean on these people for counsel at critical times in my life. These are people that love me, but are not impressed by me, and can tell me what I need to hear, not what I want to hear."

That's because life is complex and confusing, and no one individual knows everything there is to know.

In a sense, as you grow older and more mature, it's always going to be rookie season for you in some area of life. Perhaps you are starting a new job, getting married, raising kids, or confronting illness or tragedy.

What you need as you journey through life is guidance from people who can help you keep your feet on the path. You can't go it alone, because we typically want to see things the way we want to see them, not the way they really are. That's why we need people who can be painfully honest and hold up a mirror so we can see reality for what it is.

**""I try to seek out advice along the way from people who have more life experience than myself. I find it vital to lean on these people for counsel at critical times in my life. These are people that love me, but are not impressed by me, and can tell me what I need to hear, not what I want to hear."
–AARON RODGERS**

You may not face the same kind of chaos players face in the NFL, but you will undoubtedly face challenges and problems and heartbreaks that force you to your knees, and require you to reach out for guidance.

At times like those, you don't want to turn to people who don't really know you. You want to turn to those people who know you the best, who love you the most, and who have the wisdom and experience to help you face your challenges and choose the best course for your future.

When we drift from target, wise counsel can help us to recover from our errors and wrong turnings so that we can get back once more on the right path. A wise person who benefits from guidance will seek counsel before making judgment and taking action.

WHAT'S THE PAYOFF?

Choosing to seek wise COUNSEL gives me GUIDANCE to keep me on the path.

CHAPTER SEVEN

HOW ARE YOU IMPROVING TODAY?

"FORGET ABOUT LIKES AND DISLIKES. JUST DO WHAT MUST BE DONE. THIS MAY NOT BE HAPPINESS, BUT IT IS GREATNESS."

–GEORGE BERNARD SHAW

CHOOSE TO COMMIT TO GROWTH

Most people love seeing movies. Whether we're watching a new release on the big screen at the local multiplex, or sitting down in the TV room at home to watch a DVD, we spend billions of dollars every year on movie entertainment, not to mention the required snacks and goodies that go with it.

But "watching film" has a completely different meaning in the NFL. We don't watch film to be entertained. For us, it's work. The people we watch on the screen are ourselves, and we watch film to learn, to grow, and to become better players.

Are you continually improving in order to become the ideal you or are you settling for mediocrity, just getting by in life?

Adventures in the Film Room

It's a routine that happens every Monday morning at training facilities around the NFL, as players gather in the team meeting room to spend a few hours watching plays from Sunday's game.

If we had won the game, the atmosphere was typically positive and energetic. But if we had lost, the mood was more down and reserved. Either way, players knew that every play was going to be carefully scrutinized and critiqued.

That's part of why I barely slept at night after a game. Regardless of whether we won or lost, I always felt uneasy and unsettled. Typically, our offense would run about seventy plays a game. But after the game, I was not celebrating our sixty-five adequate or good plays. I was breaking down the five bad plays. And I knew that come Monday morning when we gathered to watch film, we would critique these plays even more.

After spending the morning watching film together in the team room, we would break up into groups in the afternoon for even more film critiques. Offensive line players met in one room, while the defensive line met in another. Other units of the team met in their own rooms: the quarterbacks, the running backs, tight ends, wide receivers, linebackers, and defensive backs. Even the kickers met together to watch film. (It has been rumored that they held their meetings in a janitor's closet, but I can't say for sure.)

Each one of the unit meeting rooms was equipped with all the video equipment needed to review the relevant film.

No player welcomed these film sessions. Some dreaded them. But no matter how a player felt, he knew his every move was going to be evaluated, assessed and critiqued.

Occasionally, players would be praised and applauded. If you had a game-winning or game-saving play, a coach might single you out and say, "Good job on that one." But the purpose of watching film wasn't to pass out compliments. The goal was looking for holes and weak spots that hurt the team. We were there to be critiqued.

Even if you had a pretty good game, it was safe to expect a healthy dose of critiquing. Coaches coach, and there was always something you could do better. And, if you had had a particularly bad day, or failed to do your best on a number of plays, you needed to wear your thick skin to the meeting. Remember, a poor performance not only hurts the team and reflects poorly on you, but it also reflects negatively on your coach, as well. Like it or not, you guys were linked together, for better or worse, wins and losses.

In the worst cases, you needed to get ready for being singled out, harassed and humiliated, as your performance on the field was turned into a learning opportunity for the team. And if your coaches were in a particularly nasty mood after a bad loss, they devoted a few minutes here and there to making sure everyone knew how badly you played. (The main purpose of this exercise is motivation, although I don't know if it actually works long-term.)

For NFL players, watching film is never like going to the movies. It's rarely entertaining. Most of the time, it is intimidating, depressing, frustrating, and painful.

But we do it anyway. Why? There is only one reason. We want to play better. By carefully studying both the great moments and the horrible moments from each game, we learn what went right, what went wrong, and what we needed to do to play better the next Sunday.

Some coaches call it ongoing improvement. It's all about something I call *continual growth*.

No matter who you are or what you are trying to do in your life, if you want to be good at anything, you need to learn from your mistakes and try to do a better job the next time. You may not be looking at moving images of yourself on a screen. Instead, your "film room" may be the looks of disappointment you see on the faces of your parents, your schoolteachers, your boss, or your loved ones.

"As I get older, I have begun to understand more what responsibility is and understand the true meaning of maturity and growth. True maturity is understanding your flaws and being willing to work

JARED ALLEN

"... *True maturity is under-standing your flaws and being willing to work at them to understand that your life is constantly developing. Either you are going to develop, or you're going to drift away from your goals.*"

at them to understand that your life is constantly developing. Either you are going to develop, or you're going to drift away from your goals."
–JARED ALLEN

But if you do what NFL players do and carefully examine your faults and flaws, you can learn how valuable it is to take a good hard look at your own faults and failures with brutal honesty, so you can improve things tomorrow.

Each and every one of us experiences failures. None of us is perfect. That's why continual growth is so important, because if we're not growing, we're standing still or falling backward. I choose to grow.

Be All That You Can Be

"Be All You Can Be." For twenty years, the U.S. Army used this slogan to recruit new soldiers. It was inspiring. I think we'd all like to grow, improve, and be the best we

can possibly be. But you don't need to be a soldier to commit yourself to continual growth. No matter who you are or what you do, you can work to become the very best version of yourself, even if you don't spend hours in a film room.

Going to the film room would be bad enough if Sunday games were the only film NFL players watched, but *everything* is taped, not just Sunday games. Every play in every practice is filmed, and we watch those films, too.

If I miss a block on the thirty-second play in practice, I will hear about that mistake tomorrow when we watch our practice film. If I step with my left foot first instead of my right, my error will bring me a few moments in the spotlight of shame at our next unit meeting.

The criticism players receive throughout the week can seem never-ending. You would think we would get used to it, but the fact is that nobody enjoys being criticized. Let's face it. We would rather be told how good we are than told how poorly we are doing. I think this goes back to our days in elementary school. At school, we would do crayon drawings or watercolor paintings that we would bring home to mom. The only thing we wanted mom to do was tell us, "That's beautiful, honey!" and hang our drawings on the refrigerator for all to see. We didn't want mom to critique our form or our watercolor technique.

Unfortunately, some of us have tried to apply this watercolor approach to all of life. We want people to constantly praise us, encourage us, and tell us what great people we are, and what a wonderful job we've done.

But the fact is, none of us does a great job every time. We have good days and bad days. We execute some things better than others. And frankly, sometimes we try harder than we do at other times. In the real world, not everybody gets a trophy. Somebody wins and somebody loses.

I believe that if everyone continually praised us, no matter how well or how poorly we performed, we would become lazy, proud and self-satisfied. Thankfully, there are people in our lives who will honestly tell us when our performance is poor. These people are our critics, and we should be thankful they are in our lives.

> **"When you have an injury and you go to a doctor, you don't just tell him about your minor injuries, you also tell him about the major injuries. It's the same in life. I speak on a weekly basis with my mentors, and I tell them about my major problems that I deal with in my life. They are like spiritual doctors for me."**
> **–TROY POLAMALU**

It's like Benjamin Franklin said: "Our critics are our friends, because they show us our faults."

Not everyone appreciates critics, and that includes players in the NFL. I was always amazed to see how different players responded to criticism in different ways:

Some got offended.

Some became defensive.

Some were too sensitive and became upset when their pride was punctured.

Some blamed other players or even their coaches for their poor performance.

Some experienced waves of insecurity and self-doubt.

Some felt it was completely unjust that their good plays were not praised, while their bad plays were critiqued.

Some acted out and yelled at coaches or fellow players who tried to instruct them.

Over time, I saw that the players who couldn't take criticism eventually left the NFL (asked to leave might be more accurate). But those players who could receive criticism and use it to improve their game would stick around. They were the winners. They were the players who were committed to continual growth.

> **"It's a spiritual level battle. Even warfare. You have to be courageous and bold and you can be a great warrior in that battle by recognizing where the attacks are coming from. They're not coming from the person. The person is not the problem. I have learned to confront everything and not anyone. Battles are won by fighting the problem, not the person."**
> **–JOHN HARBAUGH**

Over the years, I wrote down many quotes and thoughts about growing through criticism in my big notebooks. Here are a few:

Struggle is a requirement for growth.

Failure is the best teacher.

My goal in football was to be the very best player I could possibly be. Now that I am no longer in the NFL, my goal is to be the very best person I can be in all areas of my life. If I want to achieve this goal, I know I need to listen to criticism.

Of course, not all criticism is valid. Some people are critical 24/7, regardless of the circumstances. Some people are moody or like to hurt other people. I have found that criticism from people like this is rarely very helpful.

But I know I need to listen to critics when they have a valid point because they often can see things I can't see.

Can I tell you a secret? I don't take failure well. Who does? But if you want to be the best you can be, the ideal you, you need to listen to your critics, not get defensive about what they say.

Sure, there are times when it seems that there is more criticism than praise in life. Now you know what it's like in the film room!

The way I see it, all of life is like a big film room. Criticism is never-ending. And the sooner you realize it, then learn how to deal with it, the sooner you can learn to grow through criticism. When things got tough in the film room, I would remind myself that it was a good thing because it was making me better. I tried to get comfortable with being uncomfortable. It was holding me accountable, not just to myself, but to my coach and teammates.

One thing I tried to do was remove myself from the situation. I checked my ego at the door and didn't make it about me. Not getting emotionally involved was a very helpful coping mechanism. I focused on dealing in the truth, admitting my mistakes and learning from them. This is what a man does. There is no such thing as failure, just learning experiences.

By owning your mistakes, you actually retake the power they had over you. If you admit your shortcomings, there is nothing anyone else can say or do to affect you. When I had a bad play, I would look at it very technically. I would identify the breakdown in my technique that caused me to get beat. Then, I would resolve to do it differently the next time I was in the same situation. Because one thing is for certain in the NFL, if a pass rush move or a blitz pattern gives you trouble, opposing players and teams will see that and they will attack you the same way until you prove you can block it. That is a guarantee.

By owning your mistakes you take back your power.

The Day "My Bad" Was Really Bad

Most games in the NFL consist of 150 or 160 plays. Most of these games are highly competitive, and when they are over, you can go back and identify a small handful of plays that ultimately determined the outcome. As fans, we love to do this because it helps us give explanation to the result.

The tricky thing is, you don't know which plays are going to be these crucial ones. It could be the opening kickoff, a last second Hail Mary pass, or any one of them in between.

On some rare occasions, there is one play that sticks out above all others—where victory is snatched from the jaws of defeat, or vice versa, depending on which side you are on. This is exactly what happened on a fall afternoon in September 2006.

The Minnesota Vikings were hosting our division rival, the Chicago Bears.

The Bears were known for their aggressive defense, and there was no shortage of stars on that side of the ball. Brian Urlacher grabbed most of the headlines, but their All-Pro defensive tackle Tommie Harris was a handful as well. He played with a tremendous amount of intensity and effort. He is what we referred to as an "all-day Jesse," meaning he never took a play off. Unfortunately, I was going to experience that first-hand.

We were leading 16-12 with 6 minutes to go in the game and we had the ball. All we had to do was make a couple of first downs and the game was ours. At the very least, offensively we needed to take some time off the clock, punt, and make the Bears go the long way to score a touchdown. A field goal was of no use to them, and their mediocre offense hadn't done much against our defense all day. We were liking our chances.

It was third and nine on our own 43-yard line. We called a trap play—a quick-hitting running play. Sure, we hoped to get the first down, but it was unlikely. Chicago knew we weren't going to throw the ball and risk a clock-stopping incompletion. Our main opponent at this juncture was not the Bears, but rather the game clock. The Bears were out of timeouts, so a running play would take another 45 seconds off the clock, and bring us that much closer to victory. Many fans were hurrying toward the exits, thinking a Viking victory was a done deal. Boy, were they wrong.

On a trap play, in this case to the right, the left guard pulls to the right and "traps" the defensive tackle over the right guard, and the center blocks back on the defensive lineman that was lined up over the left guard. The play is designed to run right up the middle.

Well, I did not get "back" and block my guy, who happened to be Tommie Harris. I assumed he would play into me when he saw the guard pull, but he did not.

Tommie blew straight up the field, going a million miles an hour, and he hit our running back, Chester Taylor, at the same time he was receiving the handoff from our quarterback,

"I resolved to do this: To never get beat upfield on another back block the rest of my career. What else could I do? I couldn't change the past, but I could affect the present and the future. I vowed to become the master of the back block, and that's what I did."

MATT BIRK

Brad Johnson. The result was disastrous. The ball was fumbled and recovered by Chicago. A couple plays later, the Bears threw a touchdown pass and took the lead, 22-19, which ended up being the final score.

All losses hurt, but this one more than usual for one obvious reason—I felt like I had lost the game for us. In fact, I know I did. Sure, teammates were coming up to me in the locker room, seeing that I was dejected, and offering me words of encouragement. They were patting me on the back telling me it wasn't my fault, but we all knew that it was my fault. If I had made that back block, there was a 99 percent chance we would have won that game. It's hard to win games in the NFL. My teammates had put the work in and laid it on the line. They played good enough to win, but because of my poor technique and lazy execution, we were dealing with a loss instead of celebrating a win.

The worst part was when I left the stadium, it wasn't over. I was going to replay that play, that mistake, in my head one million times that night. I wasn't going to be able to sleep a wink, and I knew this. I had to go into the facility the next day, feel everyone looking at me, and watch the film with my teammates.

Watching that tape was like watching a horror film. It was incredibly humbling to have to watch that play with my peers. But when it was over, I resolved this: To never get beat upfield on another back block for the rest of my career. What else could I do? I couldn't change the past, but I could affect the present and the future. I vowed to become the master of the back block, and that's what I did. I played another seven-plus years after that game, and every time we called a trap play in a practice or in a game, I thought of Tommie Harris. I was determined to never feel like that on a football field ever again.

I didn't feel very fortunate at the time, but I look back on that whole experience with a lot of pride. First, it was an extremely embarrassing and humbling thing to endure, but I did it (like I had any other choice). But I owned up to the mistake with the media after the game in the locker room, and to my teammates in the film room the next day. I didn't try to make excuses or deflect the blame. I took my medicine and I'm glad I handled it the way I did.

Second, I grew from that experience as a player as well. I took a failure, turned it into a learning experience, and used it to get better. I'm quite certain I'm not the first or last guy to miss a block and lose the game for his team.

If you take something negative, work on it, and turn it into something positive, you can experience continual growth, not just in your job, but in your life.

The Art of Letting Go

Talking about that game I lost brings back powerful negative feelings. The best way to describe these feelings is to compare them to the way a guy in high school might feel if he got beat up at school one day in front of all his buddies.

I felt like I had been beaten. It was not a good feeling, and I remember being in a funk for days after that loss. And for the rest of that 2006 season, whenever we ran the trap play, I felt as if all my teammates were looking at me and asking: "Are you going to do your job today?"

I didn't stay in a funk forever. I didn't allow myself to be trapped in an emotional downward spiral. My failure had been colossal, but I knew that was not the end for me. Rather, this was just another tough lesson along the road of life. It was merely one of many lessons I have learned over the years.

How can a person learn to spring back from horrible losses and embarrassing failures? For me, recovery starts with learning to let go.

Whether I'm going through a depressing day in the film room, or dealing with failures in other areas of my life, I learn what I can and move on. It's all part of what offensive line coach Steve Loney described as not being a monkey. Here's how he told the story to a group of us during practice one day:

Once upon a time, there were people who lived in a village deep in the forest. Every few days, a mean old monkey would enter the village from the forest and steal the villagers' food.

The villagers did everything they could to try and stop the monkey from raiding their food supply. But nothing ever worked because the monkey was agile and cunning. Time after time, the monkey snuck into their village and stole their food.

Then one day, one of the village elders came up with a plan. He took a clear glass milk bottle and put a little bit of the monkey's favorite fruit down in the bottom. The next day, when the monkey entered the village, he saw the fruit and reached into the bottle to grab it.

But the opening to the bottle was too small for the monkey to get his hand back out when he was clutching the fruit. The monkey became consumed with the challenge. When he was wrestling with the bottle, one of the villagers silently snuck up behind him and bonked him on the head with a club. That was the end of the monkey and the end of the villagers' problem.

"It's the same way with you guys sometimes," said Loney. "You miss an assignment on a play, or you blow a block, and things go bad. But instead of getting up, dusting yourself off, and getting ready for the next play, you keep thinking about that last play, replaying it in your head over and over until you can think of nothing else. And then you mess up the next play."

His lesson was simple: Don't be the monkey. Let things go.

Sure, you need to learn from your mistakes, but don't let your mistake on one play keep you from being your best on the next play. Don't use your

"I love to read. I love books that inspire and books that make you think. Reading books based on the truth is a quick way to grow and learn principles for your life."

ANQUAN BOLDIN

own failures to torture yourself. Move on and do better the next time.

Being Grateful

Another thing that helps me recover from the pain of failure is developing an attitude of gratitude. That means being thankful for the good things in my life. Even after my bad play lost us the game against the Bears, I thanked God for giving me the privilege of playing in the NFL. Expressing that gratitude helped lessen my regret about losing the game.

I wrote this in my notebook almost every day of my career:

I get to be a professional football player today. What a blessing. What a gift.

When you lose a big game, it's easy to let your negative feelings color the rest of your life. That's when you need to gain a fresh perspective by taking a look around and seeing all the good things you have.

Go volunteer at a soup kitchen or the local shelter. Take a mission trip to a Third World country. Count the people in your life who you know love you. Are you alive and breathing? Then give thanks for the gift of life.

Each one of us experiences failures, and sometimes the memories of these failures stay with us a long time. That's OK as long as we learn from them, but we can't take these things personally, or let them keep us from being our best.

When bad stuff happens to you, let go! Stop reliving the past. Rip off the rear view mirror and throw it away. Just let go, and commit yourself to doing better the next time.

"I love to read. I love books that inspire and books that make you think. Reading books based on the truth is a quick way to grow and learn principles for your life."
—ANQUAN BOLDIN

Profiles in Continual Growth

In 2007, the Vikings drafted Adrian Peterson in the first round. It didn't take long for me to see why people nicknamed him AD. The nickname stands for "All Day" and it describes Peterson's legendary work ethic.

Fans knew Peterson as the running back who was named NFL Offensive Rookie of the Year. He was the guy who set the NFL record for most rushing yards in a game with 296 yards against the San Diego Chargers.

I got to see a side of Peterson no one outside the team ever saw when I witnessed his dedication to hard work in the weight room.

It was December, and Peterson's body had been bruised and battered. Guys that carry the ball in the NFL take a beating. Everybody would have forgiven him for taking it easy. But there he was in the weight room, doing squats with 315 pounds on the bar. And these were full squats, not the halfway ones some guys try to get away with.

People think players like Adrian are born gifted, and maybe they are. But he showed me through his work ethic that he was fully committed to continual growth.

O. J. Brigance was a linebacker who won championships in both the Canadian Football League and the NFL. He was also a great man off the field, serving groups like Habitat for Humanity. But it was when O.J. was diagnosed with ALS in 2007 that his character was tested as never before.

I met O.J. when I joined the Ravens. By that time, he was in a wheelchair, but he could still talk. He always told us: "Never complain and don't waste time." I watched O.J. over four years as his condition deteriorated, but he never lost his fighting spirit.

By the time I left the

Ravens, he had lost the ability to speak, but he still encouraged players by using a computer speech device like the one used by scientist Stephen Hawking. Even though his diagnosis was terminal, O. J. came to work every day to help and serve the players. He was still loving life and striving to be a better man every day.

Life's Big Film Room

What would happen to you if you spent every Monday looking at film of your performance from the last week? What if you could take a close look at how you handled the situations you faced in sports, at school, at work, and in the important relationships in your life?

You would probably see some things in the film that you weren't too happy about. That's great! If you have desire and a commitment to continual growth, you want to see your performance so you can constantly evaluate it and make all areas of your life better.

That's the only way you can become the ideal you!

We must continually practice self-assessment, including reminders of identity and purpose, refinement of character, and constant connection with true power, so that when our name is called, we are prepared to be at our very best.

WHAT'S THE PAYOFF?

Choosing to commit to GROWTH gives me SELF-IMPROVEMENT to become the very best version of myself.

CONCLUSION

THE CHOICES ARE YOURS

Thank you for reading this book. You've heard plenty from me in the previous pages, so I won't drone on and on here at the end.

Instead, let me ask you a simple question: How are YOU going to answer the questions we have posed in this book?

One person can hear something and put it into action, but another hears the same thing and doesn't do anything about it.

My hope and prayer is that you will seriously consider the seven questions posed in this book, maybe even write them down on a card you can hang on your mirror, or tape them on your computer screen, or in a place where you will see them every day. Or like me, take a small spiral notebook and stick it in your backpack. Write down your thoughts from time to time. Soon enough, some answers and choices will become clear to you.

From there, I hope you would translate the concepts we have discussed into action steps you can use to integrate these lessons into your life. If you do that, I will be thrilled, plus more importantly, I truly believe you will be much better off.

A FINAL MESSAGE

For four years I played alongside Ravens free safety Ed Reed, a great player who has been named an All-Pro eight times in his career.

During those four years, Ed had a piece of paper hanging in his locker. I noticed the paper hanging there every day I walked past it, but I never really took the time to stop and read it until my very last day in the locker room before I retired from the team.

On that final day, I took a cell phone photo of the paper in Ed's locker. Here's what it said:

"Our deepest fear is not that we are inadequate.
Our deepest fear is that we are powerful beyond measure.
It is our light, not our darkness, that frightens us.
We ask ourselves, who am I to be brilliant,
gorgeous, talented, and fabulous?
"Actually, who are you not to be? You are a child of God.
Your playing small does not serve the world.
There is nothing enlightened about shrinking so that
other people won't feel insecure around you.
"We were born to manifest the glory of God.
That is within us, it's not just in some of us,
it's in everyone. And as we let our light shine, we
unconsciously give other people permission to do the same.
And as we are liberated from our own fear,
our presence automatically liberates others."
–MARIANNE WILLIAMSON

The questions we have explored in this book can liberate you from your own fears and help you to manifest the greatness that is within you. Take a few quiet moments, and think about your answers to the seven questions:

1. Who are you?

2. What is your purpose?

3. What kind of person do you want to be?

4. Where are you going?

5. Where can you find strength greater than yourself?

6. Who can give you guidance?

7. How are you improving today?

I know that having my own answers to these questions gives me confidence, strength, and peace.

I'll close with a quote I recall a from the Greek mathematican and philosopher Pythagoras, who found his way into my college textbooks:

"Choices are the hinges of destiny."

Choose well!

Matt Birk

January 2014

AFTERWORD

The Seven Choices you were introduced to in this book can bring your spirit alive, and awaken the culture of an entire organization. It can create a spark of encouragement that will literally set your life, even an entire company, on a trajectory for greatness.

We invite you to visit our website at allprowisdom.com where you can access our resources. There you can connect with Matt and Rich. Please consider how we may be able to serve you, serve your organization, speak about the Seven Choices, and if you should desire, introduce our workshops to your leadership team.

VISIT OUR WEBSITE

ALLPROWISDOM.COM

ACKNOWLEDGMENTS

Commissioner Goodell, our thanks to you for your early support of our vision, for helping launch this work, and for your ongoing encouragement in sustaining this project. We are grateful. To the great team at the NFL office: Jeff Pash, Greg Aiello, and Dolores DiBella we thank you for helping facilitate our work with all your constituents. Ted Cuizio at the Associated Press, thank you for your positive spirit and assistance with the photo selection.

To Aaron, Anquan, Troy, Jared, Adrian, Jason, Joe, and Coach Harbaugh; each of you graciously gave of your time for the interviews, and inspired us with your thoughtful words and inspirations. Your insights bring life and visibility to the truths we are advancing. A special shout out to the Public Relations professionals who made the connections for us: Kevin Byrne, Chad Steele, and Patrick Gleason (Ravens); Bob Hagan, Tom West, and Jeff Anderson (Vikings); Tom Fanning (Packers); Burt Lauten (Steelers); Rich Dalrymple (Cowboys); and Bob Lange (49ers).

To Steve Rabey, writer extraordinaire, for capturing our voices and especially the spirit of our work. To the dream team at the Jenkins Group for your encouragement, counsel, and hard work in bringing this book to press. You have exceeded our expectations.

Finally, at a very personal level, we acknowledge and thank our friends and confidantes who have walked with us step by step, provided guidance, and offered us their counsel: Paul Vitale, Charlie Nickoloff, John Crudele, Wayne Waldera, Bob Birk, Mark Joerger, and Thom Winninger.

"Plans fail for lack of counsel, but with many advisers they succeed." Proverbs 15:22

ABOUT THE AUTHORS

MATT BIRK is a champion on and off the field. He is a Harvard graduate, and an unlikely football success story. Matt worked hard, made good choices and was guided by his conviction to become the best. As an All-Pro football center, Super Bowl Champion and NFL Man of the Year, Matt played more than 200 NFL games, inspiring players, coaches, and fans through his powerful example of making choices that to lead a great life. He and his wife Adrianna are the parents of six beautiful children under the age of eleven, and reside in Naples, Florida.

RICH CHAPMAN and Matt came together as next-door neighbors in Minnesota. An influential business and community leader, Rich brings more than twenty years of success in mobilizing, equipping, mentoring and energizing organizational leaders. An NCAA All-American in his own right, Rich has grown companies, taken one public, and inspired many through his unique ability to engage others in creating their own success. Rich, his wife Jayme and their four children are from St. Paul, Minnesota.